PENGUIN BOOKS
DERA SACHA SAUDA
AND GURMEET RAM RAHIM

Anurag Tripathi is an investigative journalist with sixteen years of experience spanning print, electronic and digital media. He has worked as editor, reportage, at Newslaundry, and senior associate editor, *Tehelka*. He started his career with the *Hindustan Times*, Lucknow, and has worked with the *Times of India*, Aaj Tak, India TV and NewsX.

In the course of his career, besides Operation Jhootha Sauda, Anurag's investigations have included busting an AK-47 arms racket in western Uttar Pradesh, exposing corruption in the power sector in Andhra Pradesh, unravelling a drug racket run by an MLA in Lucknow, and bringing to light the issue of fake caste certificates in Uttar Pradesh—and these have had on-the-ground impact in the form of official inquiries and government action.

DERA SACHA SAUDA

AND GURMEET RAM RAHIM

A DECADE-LONG INVESTIGATION

ANURAG TRIPATHI

FOREWORD BY HARTOSH SINGH BAL

PENGUIN BOOKS

An imprint of Penguin Random House

PENGUIN BOOKS

USA | Canada | UK | Ireland | Australia
New Zealand | India | South Africa | China | Singapore

Penguin Books is part of the Penguin Random House group of companies
whose addresses can be found at global.penguinrandomhouse.com

Published by Penguin Random House India Pvt. Ltd
4th Floor, Capital Tower 1, MG Road,
Gurugram 122 002, Haryana, India

Penguin
Random House
India

First published in Penguin Books by Penguin Random House India 2018

Copyright © Anurag Tripathi 2018
Foreword copyright © Hartosh Singh Bal 2018

ISBN 9780143442400

Typeset in Adobe Garamond Pro by Manipal Digital Systems, Manipal

Printed at Manipal Technologies Limited, India

www.penguin.co.in

MIX
Paper | Supporting
responsible forestry
FSC® C043100

This is a legitimate digitally printed version of the book and therefore might not
have certain extra finishing on the cover.

For my mother
and Yasha and Adiya

Contents

Part III: The Long Road to Justice

Foreword

The word 'dera' literally means an encampment. In undivided Punjab, which stretched from Delhi to the north-western frontier of the subcontinent, the term acquired a religious connotation. It came to be applied to a community headed by a charismatic figure, with its own religious practices, living in a settlement marked off from the rest of the world. Today, a majority of deras in India are offshoots of Sikhism, often with practices that are considered heterodox by the Sikh orthodoxy.

By their very nature, the deras attract followers who do not find succour within the folds of orthodox religion. Some of these followers may well be those who have found that long-settled ritual observances do not fulfil their spiritual needs, but the vast majority of them tend to be those marginalized within the caste hierarchies of Hinduism and Sikhism.

In return for the semblance of dignity offered to the congregation in a dera, the devotees offer absolute devotion and loyalty to the dera head, who is the source of all authority in a community centred around him (mostly) or her (very occasionally). Within the confines of the dera, the authority of the head is complete and unquestioned. As a result, devotees, who have already conceded to the dera head the right to question and overturn established religious practices prevalent in the outside world, consider it only natural that he should have the same right to overturn what passes for normal in worldly matters.

While deras can be sources of fulfilment in many cases, they can also be places of great oppression which can go largely unchecked over long periods of time. The dera head's power over his congregation is absolute. Anurag Tripathi's book does not just narrate a stellar piece of investigative journalism, it is also a sociological text on the now-infamous Dera Sacha Sauda headed by Gurmeet Ram Rahim Singh. As the book relates, Ram Rahim was not the kind of person who could have founded a dera; he clearly lacked the spiritual depth or the religious insight this would require. But he had the practical cunning and duplicity to get himself nominated by his predecessor to the position of the head of this dera at gunpoint and build on the authority and charisma that he thus inherited. This authority over a vast and growing congregation included the way it voted, allowing him enormous political clout.

This is key to understanding why, across a period of over two decades, he got away with unbelievable acts of violence and depravity—castration, rape and murder—without alienating much of his congregation. It is also key to understanding why government authorities, rather than acting against him, ended up collaborating in his acts of crime. The media itself was complicit, and what Anurag Tripathi and colleague Ethmad A. Khan at *Tehelka*, working under Harinder Baweja, achieved was an exception in Indian journalism.

Nothing could be more damning for the media than the nature of the court verdict against Ram Rahim. The courts upheld every serious charge brought against him, charges which much of the media had largely chosen to ignore till that point, leave alone investigate them. Till the very day of the verdict, as Ram Rahim's power and wealth grew, politicians from across the political spectrum flocked to him, seeking his help in elections. Most media institutions were no better. In fact, much of the positive media coverage for Ram Rahim took place well after Tripathi and his colleague first broke the story of his crimes.

Late in August 2017, shortly after Ram Rahim was convicted, as his supporters thronged the streets of Haryana and Punjab clashing with the police, it was interesting to see the glee with which anchors from TV channels elucidated the crimes Ram Rahim was guilty of and called out the failure of the Haryana Police to secure the streets in the aftermath of the judgment. None of them referred to the fact that most channels and newspapers had been happy to run glowing interviews of the baba and give publicity to his tacky films and music videos even weeks before the court order.

Even organizations unburdened by such commercial constraints had done little to cover a story that they devoted so much time to in the aftermath of the verdict. Today, in India, good investigative journalism is rare because organizations are unwilling to give the time and backing that *Tehelka* did to journalists such as Anurag Tripathi. Such stories require journalists to spend weeks and even months on them; they require doggedness and persistence without the guarantee that all the time and effort will pay off.

Lastly, the book also illustrates why, when done well, sting journalism remains an essential component of the profession, albeit one that must be used rarely and wisely. There are some stories, such as this, where their public importance is evident and overwhelming, where the information cannot be gathered in any other way, which justifies the use of hidden cameras and the concealment of a reporter's identity.

If Ram Rahim was finally convicted, it was because of a rare conjunction of events—a local journalist who had the courage to stand up to him and paid for it with his life; women who had been raped and men who had been castrated, standing up to threats of murder to testify in the case; a CBI officer who would not be cowed down and was, in turn, backed by his chief and the prime minister of the day; and Anurag Tripathi's *Tehelka* team.

New Delhi   Hartosh Singh Bal
March 2018   Political editor, *Caravan*

Part I

Operation Jhootha Sauda

The Letter

It was a lean day in the month of April 2007. When journalists, particularly those in Delhi, talk of a 'lean day', it means nothing much is happening news-wise. After a three-year-long stint at a twenty-four-hour news channel, where I had barely survived the madness of 'breaking news', I was yet to get used to the comparatively relaxed pace at the newsroom in *Tehelka*. Political reporting never excited me, so I had chosen to be a part of the investigation team of a magazine that was known for its avant-garde investigative reports.

One of the incentives of being a part of *Tehelka*'s investigative team was the opportunity it presented of working with team leader Harinder Baweja, popularly known by her nickname, Shammy. The other, smaller incentive was a tiny but separate room that had a desktop computer and a landline phone. This room was only for members of the investigative team and was out of bounds for other employees. As a rule, any calls related to investigative stories were transferred to this room.

One such call was put through to us that day as well. The caller sounded harried and his speech was garbled. All we could make out was that he had some papers and information about a sect called 'Dera Sacha Sauda', located on the outskirts of Sirsa in Haryana. It wouldn't be possible to give all the details on the telephone, he said, and asked to meet us in person. A date, time and place were agreed on. Within a few minutes, however, he called back, cancelling the meeting. 'My life is in danger,' he said. 'I need some time to find out if I can trust you.' All we could do from this point on was wait for him to call us back.

Meanwhile, we started our research on Dera Sacha Sauda. There was barely any information about the sect on the Internet in 2007. Most of the information out there seemed to have been written as promotional material, applauding the Dera's practices, its religion of humanity, and how its chief, Gurmeet Ram Rahim Singh, was an incarnation of God. As we dug deeper, we chanced upon a news report about the murder of a journalist, Ram Chander Chhatrapati, the editor of an eveninger, *Poora Sach* (The Complete Truth), published from Sirsa. There were sketchy details linking his murder to the Dera. This was the first clue that there could be a story worth investigating here. The more my colleague, Ethmad A. Khan, and I went through the news reports, the more convinced we became that this story had a lot of 'meat' and was worth chasing.

The next two days were business as usual. We camped next to the phone, fervently hoping for a call from the anonymous caller. On the fourth day, during the post-lunch lull, the much-awaited call finally came through. The anonymous caller asked for our personal numbers and promised to get in touch soon. He did, that evening, and we fixed up a meeting at noon the next day near our office at M-Block market in Delhi's Greater Kailash-2.

Ask any investigative journalist about the one trait that is a prerequisite in their profession, and they will tell you it is patience. In cases where the source feels there is a threat to their life and where they are fighting a sinister and powerful system, the one thing they need is to be able to trust you. We knew our caller was trying to be sure about us before he took the risk of meeting us in person. We waited patiently for his call till late afternoon the next day, and called on the number from which he had called us the previous evening. As we suspected, the phone was switched off. Finally, in the evening, he called to say that he was waiting for us at a tea stall in the alley behind our office.

Dressed in a white worn Pathani suit, our anonymous caller had a face now. He appeared to be in his late fifties, of average build. He was visibly fearful when he saw us walking towards him. An initial exchange of pleasantries was followed by a long spell of silence. All this while, we could feel him still trying to gauge whether he could trust us or not.

'Dekhiye, jo main aapko batane ja raha hun, shayad us par yakeen kar pana mushkil ho. Lekin yeh sach hai.' (You

might not believe what I am about to tell you, but it is true.)

Our mysterious source was finally talking. Little did we know what we were about to get ourselves into.

The man started by asking us how much we knew about Dera Sacha Sauda and its chief, Gurmeet Ram Rahim Singh 'Insan'. We told him whatever little we had gleaned from our reading on the Internet—that Ram Rahim ran a sect where disciples were treated equally, and one of its big successes was a drug de-addiction programme. He smiled and said, 'That is what most people sitting in Delhi think about him.'

He told us that he was a distant relative of the slain journalist, Ram Chander Chhatrapati, whom we had come across in our research on the Dera. The man alleged that Chhatrapati was murdered as a direct result of publishing several exposés about the Dera and its chief, which included reports about the sexual exploitation and rape of *sadhvi*s residing within the Dera's premises. We were stunned.

Before telling us more, he handed us the facsimile of a letter and asked us to read it. It was an anonymous letter written in 2002 by a sadhvi to the then prime minister Atal Bihari Vajpayee. The contents of the letter were shocking, to say the least, and it introduced us to the illicit empire of the Dera chief.

The three-pager was written in Hindi and its subject was 'Request for probe into rape of hundreds of girls by Dera chief (Ram Rahim)'.

I am reproducing excerpts from the letter here:

I am a girl hailing from Punjab and I have been serving as a sadhvi at Dera Sacha Sauda, Sirsa (Haryana), for the last five years. There are hundreds of other girls, who serve for 16–18 hours a day at the Dera. We are being physically exploited here. Dera Maharaj Gurmeet Singh rapes girls at the Dera. I am a graduate . . . My family members are blind followers of Maharaj (Gurmeet Ram Rahim Singh). I became a sadhvi at my family's bidding.

She went on to recount the first time she was called by the Dera chief inside his *gufa* (secret cave) and raped:

Two years after I became a sadhvi, Maharaj Gurmeet Singh's close woman disciple, Gurjot, told me one night around 10 p.m. that I had been summoned to the '*gufa*' [residence of Gurmeet Ram Rahim]. As I was going there for the first time, I was elated that God himself had sent for me. When I went upstairs, I saw Maharaj sitting on the bed holding a remote control in his hand and watching a blue film on TV. Beside his pillow on the bed lay a revolver. Seeing this, I was stunned, I felt dizzy, as if the earth had moved from beneath my feet. I wondered what all was happening here. I had never imagined that Maharaj would be such a person. Maharaj switched off the TV and seated me beside him. He offered me water and said that he had called me because he considered me very dear to him. This was my first day [experience].

Maharaj took me in his arms and said that he loved me from the core of his heart. He also said that he wanted to make love to me. He told me that at the time of becoming his disciple, I had dedicated my wealth, body and soul to him and he had accepted my offering. By this logic, your body and soul are mine now, he said.

When I objected, he said, 'There is no doubt that I am God.' When I asked if God also indulged in such acts, he shot back:

1. Sri Krishna too was God and he had 360 *gopi*s [milkmaids] with whom he staged *Prem Leela* [Love Drama]. Even then people regarded him as God. This is not a new thing.

2. I can kill you with this revolver and cremate you here. The members of your family are my devoted followers and they have such blind faith in me that they are my slaves. You know very well that your family members cannot go against me.

3. I have considerable influence with the governments. The chief ministers of Punjab and Haryana and central ministers touch my feet. Politicians seek my support and take money from me. They cannot take any action against me. We will get your family members dismissed from government jobs. I will get them killed and won't leave any evidence behind. You know very well that I had got Dera

manager Fakir Chand killed earlier. No one knows anything about him till date. Neither is there any evidence of the murder. With the power of my money, I can buy politicians, police and justice.

Thus, he raped me. For the past three months, my turn comes every twenty to thirty days. Now, I realize that he has been raping other girls staying with him.

Around thirty-five to forty women living at the Dera are thirty-five to forty years old and past marriageable age. They have compromised on their lives to be at the Dera. Most of the girls are educated and have secured BA, MA, BEd degrees. But they are living a life of hell at the Dera because their family members are fanatic followers. We wear white clothes, cover heads with scarves, are forbidden to look at men and keep a distance of five to ten feet from men as per Maharaj's commands.

We appear like *devi*s [pious women], but our situation is that of prostitutes. I tried once to tell my family members that all was not well at the Dera. But they got angry with me, saying that if God's company is not worth enjoying, then which place would be? 'It seems your mind has become corrupt, recite the name of *satguru* [the real teacher],' they told me. I am helpless. I have to obey every command of Maharaj. No girl is permitted to talk to another. As per the commands of Maharaj, girls are not permitted to talk to their families even over telephone. If a girl talks about the reality of the Dera, she is punished under the commands of

Maharaj. Just a few days ago, a Bathinda girl spoke about the wrongdoings of Maharaj. She was thrashed by other women disciples. She is still bedridden at her home due to this assault. Her father has left his service as a *sevadar* [servant of the Dera]. She is not telling anyone anything for the fear of Maharaj.

Similarly, a girl from Kurukshetra district has also left the Dera and gone back home. When she narrated her suffering at the Dera to her family, her brother, who worked as a sevadar, gave up his job. When a Sangrur girl left the Dera, went home and narrated the wrongdoings at the Dera to people, the Dera's armed sevadar hooligans visited the girl's home and threatened to kill her. They warned her not to tell anyone anything about the Dera. Similarly, girls from Mansa, Firozpur, Patiala and Ludhiana districts [of Punjab] have gone back home and are keeping quiet as they have threats to their lives. Same is the fate of girls from Sirsa, Hisar, Fatehabad, Hanumangarh and Meerut, who are not uttering a word due to the muscle power of the Dera henchmen.

On the third and final page of the letter, the sadhvi made a plea to the media and government agencies to look into the matter so that the truth about the Dera could become known and justice meted out:

If I reveal my name [and] my address, my family and I will be killed. I can't keep quiet and I also don't want to die, but I want to expose the reality [of the Dera]. If a probe is conducted by the press or some government agency, forty to forty-five girls—living in utmost fear at the Dera—if they can be convinced, are willing to tell the truth.

Our medical examination should be conducted so that our guardians and the people would know whether we are still celibate disciples or not. If we are no longer virgins, it should be probed as to who violated our chastity. The truth will then come out that Maharaj Gurmeet Ram Rahim Singh of Sacha Sauda has ruined our lives.

We were shell-shocked. If the contents of the letter were to be believed, the Dera chief, who appeared to enjoy considerable political patronage, was involved in cases of rape and murder. Another shocking revelation was that the women being exploited in most cases were not supported by their own families. They were forced to live in a helpless, miserable and inhuman condition because of the halo of saintliness that surrounded one man—Gurmeet Ram Rahim.

We were soon to discover exactly how ungodly the man who claimed to be God was. After giving us a copy of the sadhvi's letter, our source proceeded to tell us about the murder of one Ranjit Singh, once a close aide of the Dera chief. According to him, after this letter surfaced in Sirsa and was published verbatim in *Poora Sach*, Ranjit Singh was killed by the Dera chief's henchmen on the suspicion that he had something to do with the letter. This was because the sadhvi from Kurukshetra mentioned in the letter was Ranjit's sister and had also been sexually exploited at the Dera.

Our source told us that the letter had been in circulation since 2002, and after being received at 7, Race Course Road, the official residence of Prime Minister Atal Bihari Vajpayee, was posted to the offices of several higher-ups in the government, including top cops in Punjab and Haryana. The letter was also posted to the office of the then chief minister of Haryana. It was Justice Adarsh Kumar Goel of the Punjab and Haryana High Court who took cognizance of the letter on 3 September 2002, and sought a report from the district sessions judge of Sirsa. District judge M.S. Sular conducted an inquiry into the allegations mentioned in the letter and submitted his report, recommending a probe by a central agency. Following this, justice Goel referred the matter to the Central Bureau of Investigation (CBI) on 24 September 2002. When the letter found its way into our hands in April 2007, the investigation was still in progress.

What baffled us was this—with a thorough probe, this story had all the elements of a journalistic scoop. And the letter had been in circulation since 2002. So why hadn't any mainstream media organizations touched it?

The man, who was still not willing to tell us his name, told us that before reaching out to *Tehelka*, he had approached several media houses, but none had taken him seriously. Journalists in and around Sirsa were reporting on progress in the case, but after Chhatrapati's murder, no one dared to speak out openly against the Dera chief. He said he was worried that witnesses in the cases of murder and rape were being intimidated by Dera henchmen, and it was a grim possibility that no one would be left to testify in court when the matters finally come up for hearing.

The extent of intimidation in Sirsa could be gauged from the fact that when the letter surfaced, Dera followers set fire to a photostat shop were some people were making copies of the letter. People were beaten up at crossroads when found in possession of the letter, our source said. *'Ek patrakaar ki motorcycle jala di is shaq par ki woh letter distribute kar raha hai. Phir usko baba ke aadmiyon nein jam kar peeta.'* (They burnt a journalist's motorcycle on the suspicion that he was distributing the letter. He was beaten up mercilessly by the baba's supporters.) So real was the threat of immediate and violent reprisal, he said, that no one in the area breathes a word about the letter any more.

Those who had suffered at the hands of the Dera chief, said the 'man with no name', had formed a kind of secret society and had even collected some money to fund their journey to seek justice. He promised to give us the contact details of some of the sadhvis who had managed to escape the Dera by scaling its walls and were in hiding. He also knew about some old aides of Gurmeet Ram Rahim who had fallen out with him and might be willing to give vital leads. But he had a precondition: *'Isse pehle ki main aapki koi aur madad karu, sabse pehle aapko apni magazine mein yeh letter chhaapna hoga.'* (Before I help you any more in this case, you will have to publish this letter in your magazine.)

Apart from the letter and details about the murder of Ranjit and Chhatrapati, our source told us about something that was thus far unheard of on such a large scale. He told us about the forced castration of some Dera disciples at the behest of its chief. This was hard to believe. He said, to our surprise, *'Woh yeh isliye karta hain ki log uske zindagi bhar ghulam bane rahe. Baba inka istemaal apni private army banane ke liye karega.'* (He does this so that people become his lifelong slaves. He will use them to form his private army.)

After a two-hour-long meeting with our nameless source, we felt we had enough information for a story on Dera Sacha Sauda and Gurmeet Ram Rahim Singh. What we needed to do now was a thorough investigation to check the veracity of his claims and the allegations mentioned in the letter.

'Dekhiye, yeh sabke bas ki baat nahin,' the man warned. *'Woh bahut powerful aadmi hai. Aap ek baar Sirsa ho kar aaiye, sab sach saamne hoga.'* (This is not an easy task. He is a very powerful man. You visit Sirsa once and you will see the truth.)

Our immediate challenge was to dig up the facts in the investigation into the rape case against Gurmeet. As our unnamed friend had revealed very little about himself, we needed to be sure about his credibility as well. Five years had already passed since the investigation was initiated in 2002, and very little had been reported about it. I took the responsibility of cross-checking the facts of the case with the CBI, while Ethmad took on the task of contacting local journalists in and around Sirsa.

We set to work immediately. From all these sources, we were able to ascertain the following: There was definitely an undercurrent of public anger against the Dera chief in Sirsa. And there was indeed a case against him that the CBI was pursuing. In December 2002, the CBI had registered a case of rape and criminal intimidation against Gurmeet Ram Rahim Singh and was likely to file a charge sheet against him in the court in Ambala by July 2007. We were informed by our sources that the agency had successfully traced the sadhvi who had written the letter and was building a strong case against Gurmeet Ram Rahim.

The timing seemed perfect, and after a detailed discussion at an edit meeting, it was decided that the letter would be published in its totality in the magazine's 2 June 2007 issue. The reaction from the Dera was as we had expected. As soon as the issue hit the stands, our phones began ringing non-stop. Most of the callers threatened to sue the magazine. The usually one-way conversations would be laced with the choicest abuses. We were told our office would be burnt down. Their 'God' had been challenged and they would go to any extent to make *Tehelka* bleed. Letters to the editors were of a similar nature. Reports of bundles of the magazine being burnt on the road in Sirsa and other parts of Haryana poured in. Vendors were threatened with dire consequences. The pattern was akin to what Dera followers resorted to when Chhatrapati had published the letter in *Poora Sach*.

These reactions from the Dera followers only reinforced our belief that this was one story worth pursuing.

'Welcome to Sirsa'

Our nameless source had provided us enough dope on Dera Sacha Sauda in our very first meeting. Though most of the leads were not substantiated by documentary evidence, it was enough to produce a rush of adrenaline in an investigative journalist. We had several rounds of meetings with our investigation team head and after evaluating the risks and the tenacity needed for the operation, we got the green signal. The investigation was named 'Operation Jhootha Sauda', appropriate given that our aim was to unmask the spurious '*sach*' (truth) being peddled by the Dera. A two-member team was formed to execute the operation—Ethmad and I.

In the mid-noughties, hidden cameras used by journalists to carry out stings were not very sophisticated. The two cameras that were most commonly in use during that period were the 'button camera' and the 'planner camera'. To wear a button camera, you needed a customized shirt on which the camera would be glued to the second button from the top. The button was attached to a thin wire, which, in turn, was attached to an electronic recorder the size of a pager. The planner camera had the main recorder fitted into it by cutting a square into the pages at the centre, and the recorder and the pinhole camera were fixed to the spine of the planner. Both types of camera would heat up very fast and the battery fitted into the recorder would also get discharged quickly. The key to a successful sting operation was to switch the camera and recorder on only when one was very sure that something substantial would be recorded.

Ethmad was well versed in using these devices. He had done some groundbreaking investigations using these cameras; for instance, in the Nithari case. I, on the other hand, was seeing these cameras for the first time. How to place them so as to get a clear picture, how to conceal the wire of the button camera, how to ensure that it was recording while conducting a sting were alien concepts to me at the time. Thanks to the investigative team at *Tehelka*, within two days, I was trained in handling the devices and was able to record with them fairly well.

Getting the technology right was just the first step. A greater challenge was finding a convincing cover story for our presence in Sirsa. Given the notoriety *Tehelka* had already earned through its various exposés, it was virtually impossible to say to anyone giving us details about the Dera that 'we are from *Tehelka*'. Also, *Tehelka* had become synonymous with investigations, and in this case, the stakes were high. Our lives were possibly in danger. We were expressly instructed to conceal our identity and reveal it only when we were completely sure that doing so would not land us in a life-or-death situation. In short, no one was to be trusted without being doubly sure of their intent.

After another round of brainstorming, we came up with a viable cover. We were to pose as research scholars who were keen to know what drives people to organizations like Dera Sacha Sauda. Our *Tehelka* identity cards were hidden within the deepest pockets of our rucksacks. We were expected to use aliases as and when required. After getting two mobile numbers, to be used exclusively for the investigation, we were all set for the grim task before us— to explore the shadowy empire of a fake godman.

After bidding goodbye to our families and telling them that we would be on tour for a long duration, we set out for Sirsa in a hired taxi. It was the first week of May 2007. The 270–km journey on National Highway 9 (NH-9) was filled with a particular kind of nervous energy. We both kept fidgeting, our moods swinging between doubt and optimism. By the time we reached Sirsa's bus stand at 8 p.m., we had already discussed, discarded and reinvented several plans to start the investigation.

Immediately, two things struck us—the number of liquor vends, and stickers with the Dera's signature mantra—*'Dhan Dhan Satguru, Tera Hi Aasara'* (We Thank with Reverence the Supreme Lord, We Solely Depend on Him)—pasted on every second commercial vehicle at the bus stand. We stopped at a tea stall where a banner prominently displayed the same mantra. While sipping our tea, we casually inquired about it. The tea stall owner, a stout man in his late thirties, was at first offended by our query. On realizing that we were new to the city, he said, 'Sirsa is all about the Dera and this is our sect's mantra.' He said that most of the commercial vehicles there were owned by the Dera disciples and the slogan worked as a free pass to any place in and around Sirsa.

It was our first brush with the might of Gurmeet Ram Rahim Singh. 'Welcome to Sirsa,' Ethmad whispered to me.

While looking for a hotel near the bus stand, we found, not unexpectedly, that a majority of them too were either owned by Dera followers or by those who held Gurmeet Ram Rahim Singh in high regard. We checked into a hotel a few kilometres from the bus stand. Fortunately for us, the hotel was small and cheap enough not to take the rule of submitting ID proof very seriously. We were able to check in as research scholars from Varanasi. Though the hotel displayed none of the signs that we had come to associate with the Dera in our short time in Sirsa, while going to our room, up the stairs, we encountered a life-sized portrait of Gurmeet Ram Rahim Singh. At that moment, we realized that in Sirsa, it was virtually impossible to ever step out of the sphere of influence of the Dera and its omnipresent chief.

The next day, we began with a recce of the area around what is known as the 'new Dera'. We asked the staff at the hotel for directions and were told that a 7-km stretch heading towards Begu village from one of the main crossroads of Sirsa, Shah Satnam Chowk, would lead us to the Dera.

When we reached Shah Satnam Chowk, it became clear that the city was divided into two unequal parts. One half was inhabited by regular residents and was like any other town in Haryana or Punjab, but in the other, acres of land on both sides of the road leading to the Dera headquarters were completely dominated by its followers. Just a few metres down the road towards the headquarters would give you the sense that you had entered the personal fiefdom of a ruler. We had a sense of the kind of clout the Dera had in Sirsa, but nothing in our wildest imagination could have prepared us for the empire that awaited us. Be it any shop or house, on either side of the road leading to the Dera, every building was plastered with the sect's mantra, 'Dhan Dhan Satguru, Tera Hi Aasara'. The products sold in grocery shops had the logo of Dera Sacha Sauda. Every single product, from toothpaste to comb to hair oil, every business, from hair-cutting salons to bicycle-puncture-repair shops, was owned by Dera followers. People were greeting each other with the Dera salutation, which was their sect's chant. It felt surreal.

As luck would have it, close to the old Dera en route to the headquarters, all of a sudden there was a flurry of activity around us on the road. People began lining up on both sides. We saw a company of private commandos, all dressed in black and on motorcycles, ride past us. 'Pitaji' would be passing soon, they announced, asking people to clear the road and line up on the side for his 'darshan'. People in the thousands poured out on to the road from their homes and places of work. We too decided to watch the spectacle unfold. A luxury car fitted with a hooter followed within a few minutes of the commandos and headed towards the main city road. We were told that this was a pilot car that led the convoy of the Dera chief.

Within another minute, we were to witness a scene that till then, we had only seen in Bollywood films.

The fleet rushed by at high speed, flanked on either side by the Dera's private army of sevadars, all dressed in black. Before we could come back to reality, the Dera chief had whizzed by. We were later told that Pitaji was on his way to a 'Naam Charcha' in Kurukshetra. 'Naam Charcha' was the sect's term for congregations hosted generally by wealthy disciples in different cities, in order to increase the Dera's influence and induct new members. We were informed that it was difficult to pinpoint the luxury car in which the Dera chief was travelling and if one was lucky enough, Pitaji would roll down his window and give darshan.

After we had sufficiently recovered from the spectacle of the cavalcade, we got on a local tempo commonly known as a 'jugaad' (quick-fix) tempo and asked the driver to drop us at the 'old Dera', which was established on the Sirsa–Bhadra road by Shah Mastana Balochistani on 29 April 1948 (as per the Dera records). The old Dera building looked like a fortress, with its high walls and huge gates. Not much activity was happening there and only about a handful of disciples were about. The Dera chief's private army–type commandos were guarding the gates. We approached the guards and asked them if we could go in.

Then a burly guard said, *'Yahan abhi allowed nahi hain andar jana. Naye Dere par jao.'* (Entry here is not allowed as of now. Go to the new Dera.)

Four kilometres down the road, we reached the new Dera—the abode of Gurmeet Ram Rahim Singh. This Dera was even more fortified than the old one. When we expressed our desire to get in, we were told that we first had to join the sect, which was impossible to do in a day. The guards, perhaps used to curious visitors, asked us numerous questions about who we were and what our interest in the Dera was. We had worked on our cover extensively, and were able to convince them that we were research scholars. To our surprise, they guided us to a hall meant for common Dera followers, next to the main gate. We were told to stay there and not move beyond the hall. Here, we learnt that the Dera chief also owned a private TV channel, on which his sermons were beamed day in, day out on screens installed at various points around the Dera. We had had enough for the day and after spending some time in the hall, we headed back to the city.

Our priority now was to shift to a hotel closer to Shah Satnam Chowk for easy access to the Dera. Fortunately for us, the hotel we found this time did not seem to have any affiliation with the Dera. It was to be our base for almost the entire duration of our investigation. That evening, as we prepared to retire for the day, our still anonymous contact sent a text with the phone number of Ram Kumar Bisnoi.

We immediately dialled the number. Bisnoi responded, saying that there was a grave threat to his life and if at all we were to meet, it had to be at his home in Ganga village in Sirsa district. So afraid was he of the Dera henchmen that he flatly refused to travel to Sirsa city. We agreed, and the next day, boarded a bus to his village, 54 km away.

As promised, Bisnoi, a man in his mid-fifties, met us at the village bus stand. Exuding warmth and hospitality, he insisted that we first have lunch with him before any further conversation about the Dera chief. After a quiet lunch at his home, Bisnoi asked us to go with him to a pucca room near his fields. 'We will be able to talk freely,' he said. What he then told us was the story of a lone man fighting powers far greater than him, with little or no hope of success.

'Fakir Chand was not only my neighbour, he was like my brother,' he began, with tears in his eyes. 'For the last seventeen years, I have been fighting with all my limited resources to get his murderers arrested.'

According to Bisnoi, Fakir Chand was the manager of the Dera before Gurmeet Ram Rahim took over as its chief on 23 September 1990. 'Fakir was very close to the former Dera head, Shah Satnam. From an ordinary Dera follower, he rose to the rank of manager because of his hard work and dedication to the sect,' he said. 'He had no children. He sold everything, and along with his wife, settled down at the Dera. His wife passed away in 1985. It was at his insistence that I became a follower of Sant Satnam.'

In 1991, a few months after Gurmeet Ram Rahim took over the reins, Bisnoi says he got to know that Fakir Chand had gone missing. He had already stopped visiting the Dera after Gurmeet took over, but in 1991, when he went to meet his friend, he was told that Fakir had left the Dera. He was never seen again.

'It was then that I realized there was something amiss,' he said. As far as he knew, Fakir Chand was handling the Dera's finances and it was possible that his so-called disappearance had something to do with the fact that he had all the details of the Dera's resources and properties. Bisnoi told us that this information was based on what some Dera followers, who had been close to Fakir Chand but were not willing to come on record, had told him.

When Bisnoi approached Sirsa's superintendent of police (SP) in 1992, after gathering enough information from his sources, the SP refused to register a case of murder and instead asked him to file a 'missing persons' complaint for Fakir Chand. Bisnoi again filed a complaint in January 1993 with higher police officers, but nothing moved forward in the matter. 'I filed a third complaint in 2004, but in vain,' said a dejected Bisnoi.

He told us that in his view, the police would often appear to act as a stooge of the Dera. 'A few days after I lodged the complaint in 1992, some Dera followers accused the police of killing a follower, Kalu Ram. They laid siege to the police station and burnt all the records, which included my complaint. This pressure tactic proved successful. Later, the police did not register a case despite my making several requests.'

After relentlessly pursuing the case over the years, Bisnoi said he had come across a few people who admitted to him that Fakir Chand was tortured before being murdered at the behest of the Dera chief, but no one was willing to come forward. 'He is like the mafia. He will get anyone killed. Police and politicians are in his pocket.' There had been attempts by Dera henchmen to muffle his voice too, and this was the reason Bisnoi rarely ventured out of his village.

Bisnoi, like our nameless source, also told us about Ranjit Singh. It was he who managed to source the address of Ranjit's house in Kurukshetra. 'You should meet his family; they might come on record and speak about Fakir Chand's murder too,' he said, a note of desperation in his voice.

Armed with Ranjit's address and with a promise to Bisnoi to do our best, we headed back to Sirsa city.

Ranjit's home was in Khanpur Kolian in Kurukshetra, roughly 220 km from Sirsa, on the border of Kurukshetra and Karnal districts. The village is known for its prosperous farmers, such as Ranjit's family. Almost everyone we asked knew Ranjit's father, Joginder Singh, and it wasn't difficult to find his house—a palatial two-storey place that wore a deserted look.

After we rang the bell several times, a tall man opened the gate. It was Joginder Singh, once a loyal Dera follower, now a broken man. The ordeal he had gone through seemed etched on his face.

He invited us in but refused to say anything on record because he didn't trust journalists any more. Moreover, the matter was already under investigation. We seemed to have hit a wall. But, before he asked us to leave, he simply said, *'Poochho, kya poochhna hai.'* (Ask what you want to.)

'Ranjit was the main member of a ten-member core committee formed by the Dera chief. He was one of the closest confidants of Gurmeet,' Joginder said with an air of distaste.

His daughter joined the Dera as a sadhvi in 1999, after Ranjit's persistent requests. However, in 2000, Ranjit came to know of the sexual exploits of the chief. Thereafter, he stopped going to the Dera. He also withdrew his sister and daughter in April 2001.

'He told me many times that he had wasted his life at the Dera. In May 2000, the anonymous letter surfaced. I asked him about the veracity of the letter. He told me that whatever is written in the letter is true,' Joginder recalled.

In the letter, there was a mention of a sadhvi from Kurukshetra who had left the Dera and told her family about her sexual exploitation at the Dera. Gurmeet Singh and his henchmen suspected Ranjit to be behind the letter.

'Balwant Singh, a teacher from our village who belongs to a rationalist organization, had circulated copies of the letter in the village and this was another reason why the Dera suspected that Ranjit was behind all this.'

On 15 June 2002, Ranjit bought a life insurance policy of Rs 5 lakh as he was worried about his two daughters in case something happened to him. The same day, he told his father that Krishan Lal, manager of the Dera, had called him there the next day. Recalling how scared his son was after he got that call, Joginder said, 'He was very scared. He was awake the whole night and kept pacing. He was restless and I told him that everything would be all right. I was proven wrong.'

The following day, Ranjit went to the Dera along with his friend Subhash Khatri, and returned the same night. 'He told me he had been threatened and asked to seek Gurmeet Ram Rahim's forgiveness for the letter. He refused to do so as he maintained that he hadn't written any such letter.'

On 26 June 2002, Jasbir Singh and Sabdil Singh, the latter a police constable attached as gunman to the Dera chief, reached their house late in the evening. They repeated what Ranjit had been told at the Dera—that the chief was angry with him for the anonymous letter and that he should seek his pardon. They had come there at the order of the Dera chief, who had asked them to issue a strict warning to Ranjit.

While we were having this conversation, a young woman entered the room.

Though her father clearly instructed her not to speak, she still shared her bit. 'On 1 July 2002, Ranjit told me that Inder Sain, Krishan Lal and Avtar Singh had pressured him to beg for forgiveness from the baba and return to the Dera, else the baba would have him eliminated,' she revealed. He told Suman (name changed) that he had told the baba's henchmen that if they kept pressuring him to return to the Dera, he would tell the truth about the baba's activities to the entire *sangat* (congregation). At this point, Joginder asked her not to speak any more, but she was allowed to listen to our conversation.

'On 6 July, Jasbir Singh and Sabdil Singh came again to Khanpur Kolian, to our house, and threatened Ranjit. They said that Gurmeet Singh was furious with him about the matter of the anonymous letter, and if he still refused to apologize, they had been instructed to kill him. During this meeting, Ranjit was accompanied by his friend Mai Chand from the village,' Joginder told us.

At this point, Joginder called his son-in-law, Paramjit Singh, on the phone and asked us to speak to him. Paramjit told us that when Ranjit withdrew his sister and two daughters from the Dera, he was asked for a reason. 'The Dera is a fraud and has become a den of sexual exploitation over the years. Gurmeet was raping sadhvis residing in the Dera. He (Ranjit) confided in me that Suman had also been raped by Gurmeet,' Paramjit told us. Ranjit was worried about the future of his daughters. He rued the fact that he had wasted twenty-eight years of his life at the Dera. About fifteen days before his murder, Ranjit told Paramjit what he had also told his father and sister—that the Dera people suspected him of being behind the anonymous letter, and that he was being followed. He said he feared for his life, which would be under threat if he didn't do Gurmeet Ram Rahim's bidding.

On 7 July 2002, Ranjit Singh was shot dead in his village and his body was dumped in his own fields. 'Gods of stone are better than Maharaj Gurmeet Singh as they do not cause any harm to anybody,' said Kamlesh, Ranjit's aunt, who had come into the drawing room to collect the teacups. A fortnight before his murder, he had come to her house. 'He was pale with fear. He was an ever-smiling man, so it was unusual,' she recalled.

While recounting the torment the family had gone through and how, still, their life was in danger, Joginder broke down. We wanted to know more about the Dera, but were told that Suman had already given her statement to the CBI.

We took the mobile number of Balwant Singh, the schoolteacher and rationalist who had distributed copies of the anonymous letter, and left the house.

Balwant agreed to meet us in an old school building. As he spoke to us, his eyes shone with the determination to expose the wrongdoings of the Dera chief. 'We knew that the Dera chief was a big criminal. Our Tarksheel Society wants to make people aware of the reality of this man,' he said when we asked why he had distributed copies of the letter.

'When we got hold of the letter, we used our network to ensure that it reached the maximum number of people. This angered the Dera followers and they beat us up,' he said, recalling the day when he, along with another rationalist, Raja Ram Handiaya, was cornered on the outskirts of the village. 'They beat us up and repeatedly asked us where we had got this letter. They wanted us to take Ranjit's name.'

During our conversation, Balwant made another startling revelation. He knew a man, he said, who had been castrated at the Dera and had somehow managed to escape by scaling the boundary wall. The man was in hiding and a meeting could be arranged if he agreed.

The ambit of our investigation was expanding, and all we needed was someone to connect all the dots. Someone who was witness to the Dera chief's crimes, and was part of his core team when the alleged orders for murder, castration, and so on had been issued.

And that's when Khatta Singh, a former driver of Gurmeet Ram Rahim, made a dramatic entry. His revelations would ultimately pave the way for the beginning of the end for the seemingly all-powerful Dera chief.

Meeting Suman

Returning from Khanpur Kolian that evening, we had three things on our mind. We had information about rape and murder cases against the Dera chief. What we now needed to do was to check the veracity of the allegations of forced castration, illegal encroachment of land in and around Sirsa by Dera Sacha Sauda, and find someone who was a witness to any of the crimes committed by the fake godman.

It was also important to get in touch with a CBI officer working on the cases against Gurmeet Ram Rahim in order to find out which stage the investigation into the anonymous letter was at. For three days after our visit to Khanpur Kolian, we made no headway. We tried to connect with local journalists, but quickly discovered that they were either under threat from the Dera or appeared to be on its payroll. We got little or no information that could be of any help to the investigation. It was impossible to get information on the land-grabbing, as almost every establishment on the road leading to the Dera was owned by disciples and members of a land mafia that allegedly seemed to work under the Dera's patronage. Our one hope was our source at the CBI's Delhi headquarters, who promised to share the number of a colleague who was working on the cases against the Dera chief.

That crucial number reached us on the fourth day. It belonged to an officer who had been on the case of the anonymous letter since the day the Punjab and Haryana High Court had ordered a probe. The officer asked us to meet him in Palwal in Haryana the very next day. We hired a local taxi after doubly ensuring that the cab driver was not a Dera follower. After travelling 336 km, we met the lanky officer at a highway dhaba off NH-9, on the border of Palwal.

'We are about to nail him,' was his first response when we asked about the progress in the case. Somehow, I took an immediate liking to him. He looked like one of those officers who stand out because of their integrity and dedication to their work. He was as determined to see Gurmeet Ram Rahim punished as the Dera chief's victims, and now, we too had joined that club.

'The biggest hindrance we have faced since 2002, after this case was handed to us, is his connection with the top politicians of Haryana and Punjab,' the officer told us candidly. 'There is not a single political party whose patronage this man doesn't enjoy. Actually, it was a far bigger challenge to tackle the political pressure than it was to locate the sadhvi who wrote the anonymous letter!'

So the agency had finally tracked down the sadhvi behind the letter. That was remarkable, considering how little they had to go on.

'In 2002, after the case was handed to us, nothing was moving ahead and it seemed like a wild goose chase,' he said during our second round of tea. Despite the CBI's best efforts and repeated requests to the Dera to provide a list of sadhvis who stayed there from 1999 to 2002, the Dera management refused to cooperate. The local police was also of no help, it seemed.

'We later learnt that the Dera maintained a list of bribes paid to cops so that it could be used against them for favours as and when required,' the officer revealed. It may be noted that, in 2003, the Dera chief had even succeeded in getting a court order to stay an investigation against him which was based on the letter. The probe was halted for the better part of 2003 and 2004, after which the stay was finally vacated.

'For three years, we travelled across the length and breadth of Haryana and Punjab and worked on any small lead we received, but nothing substantial came out,' he said.

During the investigation, the agency's sleuths received information about a former sadhvi, living in a village in Bathinda in Punjab, who had left the Dera in 1999.

'We had credible information that this was the sadhvi we were looking for. However, it seems that we were misled.'

When the team reached Bathinda, the former sadhvi refused to come on record or corroborate the claims made in the letter. 'Family pressure and the fear of being eliminated was clearly written all over her face,' the officer recounted.

It was only in 2005 that the CBI managed to get a list of the Dera's residents. The list had the names of fifty-three sadhvis living in the girls' hostel adjoining the Dera, and eighty sadhvis who were living within both the old and new Dera premises. Also included were the names of twenty-four more sadhvis who had left the Dera after 1997. Out of the 133 sadhvis living at the Dera and its hostel, the CBI managed to speak to 130. Adding to the agency's frustration, none of them were willing to come on record.

'None of the sadhvis cooperated with us. They were under the complete control of the Dera chief,' the officer told us.

As questioning the sadhvis staying at the Dera yielded no results, the agency started looking for the sadhvis who had left. It took another six months for the agency to trace twenty out of the twenty-four who had left the Dera between 1997 and 2002. The CBI faced another challenge now.

'Most of the former sadhvis were now married and had children.' Family members of these former sadhvis would not allow them to be questioned by CBI officers.

'Not in one or two instances, but in most cases, the elders in the family were not willing to listen to a single word against the Dera chief. We were shocked to learn that in most of the cases, the family members blamed the sadhvis for leaving the Dera.'

The CBI examined eighteen girls who had left the Dera, some of whom did manage to convey that the Dera chief and his henchmen were dangerous and that they would have to fear for their lives if they spoke against them.

After hitting a wall numerous times, it was not until May 2006 that the CBI finally managed to convince two former sadhvis to speak on record. They gave a detailed account of the Dera chief's sexual exploitation of the sadhvis, and what happened to them in August 1999. One of them recorded her statement under Section 164 of the CrPC (Code of Criminal Procedure) in March 2007.

'Is this sadhvi from Kurukshetra?' we asked, on a hunch.

The officer confirmed with an affirmative nod. It was Suman.

We asked the officer if it was possible for him to provide us with a copy of Suman's statement. He said the matter was still under investigation and it would be going against the law if he did so, not to mention a breach of trust between the agency and the victim. However, he said that Suman or those of her family members who knew the contents of her statement were free to share the details with us independently if they wished to.

The next step had practically been decided for us. We knew we needed to travel once more to Kurukshetra, and try and win Suman's and her father, Joginder's trust, and convince them to talk to us.

During this meeting, we also learnt that the CBI was in touch with a former driver of Gurmeet Ram Rahim, and was planning to make him a witness in the murder cases of Ranjit Singh and Chhatrapati.

With a promise to let us know of any updates in the case, the officer departed. It was already late evening, so we decided to stay on in Palwal. We made plans to visit Kurukshetra to meet Suman.

The following day, we headed to Khanpur Kolian directly from Palwal. Unlike his caginess during our first meeting, this time around we found Joginder more forthcoming, especially after we told him about our meeting with the CBI officer. We told him that as the agency could not provide us with Suman's statement, it was important for us to talk to her. After some initial hesitation and telling us that his honour was at stake in the village, he finally relented, but with the rider that we could not publish her version till the case reached some sort of conclusion.

Initially a bit reluctant, Suman started narrating the horror she was subjected to during her stay at the Dera.

'I joined the Dera in 1999 as a sadhvi upon my brother's insistence.' At first, she found nothing suspicious. She was accommodated in the girls' hostel adjoining the Dera. It was called Sadhvi Niwas and housed most of the Dera's sadhvis. She was also appointed to work as a teacher at a school run by the Dera.

One day, a month into her stay at the hostel, she was told that she was required to do sentry duty at the gufa that was Maharaj's (Gurmeet Ram Rahim's) residence within the Dera. She would be up for night duty once in about twenty days. It was while she was stationed outside the gufa one night that she saw a sadhvi, Shyama (name changed), emerge from the gufa weeping.

'She was crying and seemed as if she were in a lot of pain. When I asked her what had happened, she started abusing Maharaj and said he was not a good man.' Shyama told Suman to leave the Dera as soon as she could. When Suman asked her why, Shyama clammed up and refused to say anything more.

The next day, Suman learnt that Shyama's parents had come to the Dera and taken her and her sister away. In the girls' hostel, a sadhvi confided in her that Shyama's sister had also been summoned several times to the gufa late at night by Maharaj.

This was not a stray incident, and Suman would go on to encounter many sadhvis coming out of the gufa weeping and abusing Maharaj, many of whom would go on to leave the Dera, never to set foot on it again.

Suman told us about one more sadhvi who swore at Gurmeet Ram Rahim, calling him 'rakshas' (monster) in the presence of several other disciples. Sadhvi Ravneet Kaur (name changed) and sadhvi Paramjeet Kaur (name changed), whom Gurmeet named 'Gurapple', also left the Dera—on account of his misbehaviour, it can be assumed. It was during this period that senior sadhvis would often ask her whether Maharaj had granted her 'maafi' (pardon). When she asked them what it meant, they would laugh and say that she would find out soon enough.

'This chain of events shook me to the core. I felt I should also leave the Dera, but could not because Ranjit's daughter, Ritu, was doing her BA from the college run by the Dera management,' she said.

It was during the late evening of 29 August 1999 that Suman's worst fears would come true.

'At around 8 p.m. that day, a Dera management committee member, Sudesh, told me that babaji had summoned me to the gufa. That was the first time I entered that place. I was ushered inside by one of the sentries on duty. When I went in, I saw that Maharaj was all alone there.'

Gurmeet Ram Rahim asked her to sit beside him. When she sat on the floor, as disciples were wont to do in his presence, he insisted that she sit next to him, on his bed. He began by asking her about her life before she became a sadhvi, and about her experience at the Dera. He insisted that she tell him about all the 'mistakes' she had committed in her past. When she hesitated, from a table next to his bed, he picked up a letter written by a boy and addressed to her. It had been mailed to the Dera's address in Sirsa. Gurmeet prodded her to tell him who this boy was and what sort of a relationship she had with him. She explained that he was a boy she knew from college and that she had nothing to do with him.

'Maharaj told me I need not worry about that boy and that he would be taken care of. He added that by becoming a sadhvi, I had given away my body and mind to him.'

By now, sensing the direction in which the conversation was headed, Suman wanted to flee the gufa. But Gurmeet wouldn't let her. He grabbed her, forcibly kissed her on her forehead, and began to fondle her. 'I kept protesting and resisting,' remembers Suman. To intimidate her into submission, Gurmeet began telling her about his 'connections' with top politicians and officers. He was worshipped as 'Bhagwan' and could do whatever he wished to, he said.

Desperate now, Suman told Gurmeet that she would tell her brother, Ranjit, everything. He laughed loudly and said that her brother was such a staunch disciple that he would not believe even a word uttered against Gurmeet. She repeated that she trusted her brother with her life and he would believe her.

'If that happens, I will have Ranjit killed and will bury his body so that nobody will ever come to know about it,' Suman remembered him saying. Terrified, she tried to escape his clutches. She screamed and begged him to let her go, but her pleas had no effect on the man who claimed to be God.

As a parting shot, the Maharaj warned her about discussing her rape with anyone. 'It will not be good for you or your family,' he said without mincing any words.

'I was so scared,' Suman recounted, visibly shaken even after all those years. 'I immediately went back to the hostel and wept for hours. I had no one to confide in. My faith was shattered.'

Fearing for her family's safety and reputation, she chose to keep quiet and not tell anyone about what had happened to her.

A few months passed. Life at the Dera seemed to continue as usual. However, Suman would soon find out that her ordeal was far from over. Five or six months after the first incident, the warden of the girls' hostel let Suman know that she had again been summoned to the *gufa*. Did she have a choice? She didn't think so. She couldn't possibly put her family in danger. This time, the summons came during the day. Gurmeet was waiting for her near the gufa's entrance.

She remained outside and asked him why he had called for her. According to her, Gurmeet seemed to get upset at this. He started shouting at her and tried to pull her inside the gufa. Somehow, she extricated herself and warned him that if he attempted to force himself on her, she would start screaming until someone came to her rescue. She quickly fled the scene. For a few months, she was left in peace.

About a year had passed since the first incident of rape when the dreaded summons came again, via Dera manager Paramjeet Kaur. When Suman refused outright, Paramjeet told her that she would not get food from the langar until she complied. 'This was one of the ways that sadhvis who refused to go to the gufa were penalized and tortured. Many sadhvis starved for days until they gave up and agreed to submit themselves to Maharaj.'

After being repeatedly threatened, Suman reluctantly went to the gufa.

Gurmeet was once again standing near the entrance. On seeing her, he went inside the gufa and waited for her to come in.

'Once I entered the gufa, he closed the door and started to force himself on me.' When Suman protested and said she would shout, Gurmeet laughed and said that nobody outside the soundproof chamber would hear her voice.

'I continued to plead with him, telling him that the sadhvis considered him "Bhagwan". He said that if everyone thought of him as God, then he had complete right over them and everything that belonged to them. Despite her continued protests, she was raped. While committing the act, Gurmeet told her that the outside world had rendered her '*apavitra*' [impure], and in this way, he was making her '*pavitra*' [pure] once more. He had forgiven her for whatever mistakes she had committed in her past.

This was the maafi she had heard being whispered about among the sadhvis. She had been 'pardoned'.

Suman remembered feeling completely powerless. Despite all the resistance she had put up, she hadn't been able to fend off another rape. This time too she was threatened with dire consequences if she told anybody about what had happened to her in the gufa.

This incident broke Suman's spirit. At the end of her ordeal, she somehow mustered the courage to ask Gurmeet that she either be sent home or shifted elsewhere. He seemed to acquiesce and allowed her to move to the old Dera. To her horror, she learnt that here too there was a gufa that the chief would periodically visit. In a pattern she was familiar with, here too sadhvis would be deputed to stand guard outside the gufa when Gurmeet was in residence. Sadhvis would also be summoned inside the gufa as per his mood.

Living in almost constant fear, Suman decided to break her silence when her brother came to visit her. Ranjit asked her not to talk to anybody else, including her parents. He promised he would take her and his daughters out of the Dera very soon. He did so in April 2001. Suman was married within a few months, in October that year.

Suman was first examined by the CBI on 25 February 2005. At the time, she withheld the information that she was raped twice by Gurmeet Ram Rahim.

It was during her second recorded statement to the CBI, on 27 July 2006, that Suman finally spoke up about being sexually exploited by Gurmeet Ram Rahim.

'I had not spoken about the rape in the previous statement for the sake of my family's reputation and the apprehension that my husband might divorce me,' she told the CBI. 'I mustered up the courage after the CBI arrested Dera manager Krishan Lal, one of the prime accused in Ranjit Singh's murder.'

She had taken her husband and parents into confidence, she said, and they had encouraged her to tell the truth.

As we listened to Suman, we realized that the seemingly disparate dots in our investigation were slowly getting connected. To begin with, the contents of the anonymous letter were not ambiguous in any way, and Suman had just confirmed that there had indeed been scores of rapes within the Dera premises.

We left Khanpur Kolian having assured the family that as long as the charge sheet in the case was not filed, this conversation would not be published. The family had gone through a lot. They had staked everything in their fight to bring a powerful man like Gurmeet Ram Rahim Singh to justice. We could not but respect their tenacity and their will to see justice done.

Here, I will take a detour before I write more about the investigation. During our interaction with our source in the CBI, we realized that the agency didn't think that one sadhvi's statement would be enough to nail the Dera chief. He was of the view that during the trial, Gurmeet's counsel could derail the case by saying that Suman was concocting the story of her rape because she thought that her brother had been murdered by the Dera chief. This was why the agency wanted to substantiate the rape charges against Gurmeet Ram Rahim, and establish a pattern of systematic sexual exploitation at Dera Sacha Sauda. They needed to track down the other sadhvis to make a solid case against him.

In the later stages of the investigation, I received a copy of the deposition of a former sadhvi which became the basis of the second rape case against Gurmeet Ram Rahim Singh. As we didn't meet that sadhvi during the investigation in Operation Jhootha Sauda, I am reproducing here her deposition, made before the additional sessions judge, Ambala, on 27 October 2007 (there are no changes other than grammatical editing to improve readability):

My parents are residents of Sirsa. The name of my father is Mulakh Raj. My family had been followers of Dera Sacha Sauda since the time of my grandfather.

Often, I would also accompany my father to Dera Sacha Sauda. I developed the tendency to serve the Dera and became a sadhvi. In June 1998, I became a sadhvi and started living at the Dera premises. At that time, Baba Gurmeet Ram Rahim Singh was the head of the Dera. I identify him. I have seen him on the screen of the courtroom, when he was present through videoconferencing. I used to reside at the girls' hostel at the Dera. When I became a sadhvi, Baba Gurmeet Ram Rahim Singh named me 'Nazam'.

I used to teach at the school from 8 a.m. to 2.30 p.m. From 4 p.m. to 6 p.m., I would give tuitions to children who were weak in studies. Sadhvis needed to perform duty as guards at the door from the girls' hostel to the gufa in two shifts—from 8 p.m. to 12 a.m. and from midnight till 4 a.m. By gufa, I mean the place where Baba Gurmeet Ram Rahim Singh used to reside.

In September 1999, I was stationed on duty as guard from 8 p.m. to 12 in the night outside the gate of the gufa. At around 10 p.m., Baba Gurmeet Ram Rahim Singh came out of the gufa and called me inside. I was alone on duty at that time. I went inside the gufa as I used to respect him a lot and treated him like God. I thought he must have some work to allot me.

Baba Gurmeet Ram Rahim Singh was sitting on his bed in the gufa. He asked me to sit on the bed. I tried to sit on the floor but Baba Gurmeet Ram Rahim Singh asked me to sit next to him. Then Baba Gurmeet Ram Rahim Singh asked me about myself and the Dera.

He inquired whether I was feeling at home at the Dera or not. He also inquired about the other sadhvis and I replied that they were nice.

Baba Gurmeet Ram Rahim Singh then tried to touch me. However, I restrained him from touching me. He forcibly embraced me and kissed me on the forehead. Forcibly, he made me lie on the bed and took off my clothes. He was physically very powerful and forcibly, he raped me. I started weeping while putting my clothes back on. Baba Gurmeet Ram Rahim Singh threatened me. He said that I should not disclose this incident to anyone and in case I did, it won't be good for me. After the incident, I left for the hostel. On seeing me weeping, other girls gathered around me. However, I did not disclose anything to them.

Next morning, my parents came to the Dera to attend the majlis. I met my parents and told them about the incident. After taking permission from Baba Gurmeet Ram Rahim Singh, my parents took me home in the evening. My parents and I did not report the matter to the law enforcement agencies as Baba Gurmeet Ram Rahim Singh had threatened me and he had clout with higher-ups such as politicians.

I got married to Sujan Sethi in May 2000. The parents of my husband were also followers of Dera Sacha Sauda, Sirsa. After marriage, my husband suspected my virginity. After a long time, I disclosed to my husband that Baba Gurmeet Ram Rahim Singh had raped me once.

When the investigation of this case was going on, we started getting phone calls where the callers said they were calling from the Dera and I should not appear before the CBI officer and make any statement regarding the incident. Even when the challan was presented, we used to get phone calls stating that I should withdraw my statement made before the investigating officer. A lot of pressure was exerted on me, on account of which my husband and I had to leave the house of my in-laws. My in-laws were staunch followers of Dera Sacha Sauda. Once, my husband was also taken to Dera Sacha Sauda. He was asked to withdraw our statements and sign affidavits for the same.

My father-in-law received a call from the Dera and he took me and my husband to the Dera. My husband, my father-in-law and I were made to sit in Suchkhand Hall, situated behind the place where the satsang is performed by the accused. Then we saw him sitting in a car coming towards us. He was staring at us. He said that we should continue to visit the Dera, and subsequently left.

After Baba Gurmeet Ram Rahim Singh left, a sadhu of the Dera, Mohan Singh, told us that the papers were not ready and after getting the papers prepared by the lawyers, we would be called again. My father-in-law replied that he would send us as and when we were summoned to the Dera. The next day, my father-in-law started getting telephone calls from the Dera stating that the papers were ready and that we should come and sign the same. However, we refused to sign the papers. It was then that my husband and I left our in-laws' house and started residing at the house of my parents.

The incident of rape that I have mentioned above had taken place on the premises of the old Dera.

This statement, along with Suman's, established a clear pattern. The Dera chief had created an aura around himself where his disciples thought of him as an incarnation of God. It was their faith in him that he exploited the most.

In both cases, he started with casual conversation to put his victims at ease. When his sexual advances were resisted, he would try different tactics to intimidate his victims—either by boasting about his connections with politicians or with the threat of getting the victim and her family eliminated. In both cases, he showed no remorse or pity because he assumed the victims were too meek to raise their voices.

While returning from Khanpur Kolian after our meeting with Suman, we knew we had to do whatever we could to expose the Dera chief. As we could not legally use Suman's statement at that time, our hope hinged on Khatta Singh. The CBI officer had already indicated that the agency was tracking him. It was important that we got him on record before any legal restraint barred him from speaking to the media.

Little did we know that even though we would eventually meet Khatta Singh, it would only be after countless sleepless nights and chasing him over several kilometres across Punjab and Haryana.

A Controversy Erupts

From Khanpur Kolian, we returned to Sirsa city, to the hotel that we had made our base. Khatta Singh was next in our crosshairs, the one vital link to corroborate all the allegations we had come across against Gurmeet Ram Rahim. Given the fact that the CBI was treating him as a vital witness in building a case against Gurmeet, and the fact that his life was under threat, it turned out to be next to impossible to coax our sources in the agency to part with his contact details. We turned to Sirsa-based journalists too, but with no success.

A few days later, we were sitting in our hotel room, frustrated and dejected. And that is when it struck us that we must contact Ram Kumar Bisnoi, who had already shared so much with us about his lone battle for justice for his friend, the former Dera manager Fakir Chand.

We called Bisnoi and relayed to him all the information we had managed to gather till then. If he could manage to get Khatta Singh's number from his sources at the Dera, it was quite possible that he might tell us exactly what happened to Fakir Chand, since he was Gurmeet Ram Rahim's driver at the time. Like us, Bisnoi was also desperate to get someone on the record who would give some information about his friend's alleged murder. He needed evidence that would help counter the local police's 'missing person' theory that essentially diluted the case.

Over the years, Bisnoi had managed to establish contact with several Dera followers who were disillusioned with the chief. This network would come in handy now to trace Khatta Singh. We asked Bisnoi to proceed with utmost caution since even a word about Khatta Singh's association with the CBI and journalists could jeopardize his and his family's lives. Bisnoi too knew that he had to choose his source within the Dera wisely.

While we waited for Bisnoi's call, we used the time to dig into the land-grabbing accusations against the Dera (details in a later chapter). It took Bisnoi all of two days to track Khatta. He gave us two mobile numbers and said, 'Khatta Singh keeps alternating between these two numbers. And he rarely picks up a call from an unknown number. You can try your luck.'

Buoyed by the fact that we at least had a lead on Khatta, we took a deep breath and dialled both the numbers one by one. Little did we know at that time that chasing the man was going to be a Herculean task. Both the numbers were switched off. We kept trying both the numbers at regular intervals, only to hear the telecom operator's prerecorded message, 'This number is switched off, please try later.'

By the evening, we'd decided to send an SMS to both numbers: 'Urgent. Call us back. Your friend.'

We just hoped that he would see the text message when the mobile was switched on and there was a slim chance that he might call us back. Deep within, we were battling a growing hopelessness. The success of Operation Jhootha Sauda depended on this man. Both his mobile phones were switched off. And we had no other way to contact him.

We spent a sleepless night, obsessively checking our mobile from time to time. We finally dozed off at the first light of dawn. When we opened our eyes some time later, we were aghast to see a missed call at around 5.30 a.m. from one of the numbers. Immediately, we tried calling back, only to find the number switched off once more. Kicking ourselves for falling asleep at the most inopportune moment, we spent another sleepless night thinking that he might call. But our luck seemed to have deserted us.

For two more days, Khatta eluded us like a desert mirage. We took to staying awake even during the early morning hours, just in case he tried to call. We had already been in Sirsa for more than two weeks. We called our office and asked our boss whether we should return to Delhi and collate all the information that we had, even as we kept trying to contact the elusive Khatta. We must have sounded dejected and even a bit desperate, but words of encouragement from our editor and a 'yes' to our request renewed our resolve to stay on a bit longer and keep up our efforts to track Khatta. Meanwhile, we kept visiting the Dera incognito.

Finally, after three more days of calling relentlessly, Khatta finally called us. This time, we were not napping.

'*Aap kaun hain aur mujhe message kyon kar rahe hain?*' (Who are you and why are you sending me messages?) A hint of fear was perceptible in the caller's voice. When he spoke, his voice quivered. He was nervous.

We told him that we were on his side and were pursuing cases against the Dera chief. He said that he was already in touch with the CBI and would not be able to divulge any details. He asked us twice whether we were calling him on behalf of the Dera chief. To put his mind at ease, we thought it best to let him know that we were friends of Bisnoi's, who was pursuing Fakir Chand's case and that we wanted to help him.

'I don't believe you,' was Khatta's immediate response. We were nonplussed. 'And I can't disclose where I am, nor can I meet you. My life is in danger.'

'We have already met Ranjit's father as well as Bisnoi,' we said. 'You can check whose side we are on.'

He disconnected the phone without letting on whether what we had said had cut any ice with him. We decided to give him some time to think.

Two days and several calls later, Khatta picked up the phone. This time, he sounded less suspicious about us.

'*Dekho, meri jaan khatre mein hain, baba mujhe marwa dega agar usko pata laga ki main uske khilaaf bol raha hun.*' (Look, my life is in danger. Baba will have me killed if he finds out that I am speaking against him.) Despite being in touch with the CBI, he said, he still feared for his life.

He had inquired about us and had verified that we had indeed gone to meet Joginder in Khanpur Kolian as well as Bisnoi. Khatta said that he knew too many of Gurmeet Ram Rahim's secrets, and this was why the Dera chief and his men were after him.

We requested him to meet us once. 'I will decide the place, time and date and let you know,' he said, before disconnecting the call.

The next day, at exactly the same time, Khatta called and told us to leave for Panipat without any delay. Once we reached there, we were to call him to find out where we were to meet. We hurriedly organized a taxi and headed towards Panipat, which is roughly 211 km from Sirsa. And so began a cat-and-mouse game.

After travelling nonstop for five hours, we reached the bus stand at Panipat, from where we duly called Khatta Singh. He asked us to wait there for some time while he found a safe place for us to talk.

It was two hours later that our phone rang. It was Khatta, who said, '*Yahan bahut khatra hai. Mil nahi paaunga. Aap Sirsa laut jao. Kal baat karta hun.*' (It is too risky here. Won't be able to meet. Please go back to Sirsa. Will call tomorrow.)

Before we could say anything, he disconnected the call and switched off his phone. We were crestfallen. It felt like we had been taken for a ride. But then, we realized we were dealing with a man who faced a very real threat to his life. He was obviously not going to act rationally or calmly. His paranoia was understandable, we reasoned, trying to place ourselves in his stead.

While driving back to Sirsa that evening, we called Bisnoi and narrated the incident to him. What Bisnoi then told us gave us a better idea of Khatta's state of mind.

'Baba knows that Khatta was in touch with the CBI,' said Bisnoi. 'His henchmen are searching for Khatta in all the places and locations that he could be found in Haryana and Punjab.'

Bisnoi also advised us to tread cautiously, as chasing Khatta might possibly result in our cover being blown. We decided to take it easy and stay put in our hotel the next day.

After waiting for a day, we called Khatta again. This time, when we spoke to him, we wanted to know whether he was just buying time by leading us on—something that would derail the investigation.

'You want to talk or not?' I asked him bluntly. He must have sensed the irritation in my tone. He tendered an apology for cancelling the last meeting, which he'd done because, he said, the CBI had hinted to him that a spy from the Dera had discovered his hiding place in Panipat. He said that when he was coming to meet us at the bus stand, he had spotted two Dera loyalists following him. He'd had to give them the slip and leave the city at the earliest.

He then gave us the address of a small dhaba on the Palwal highway and asked us to meet us there in two days' time. We were to reach there by noon and tell the dhaba owner that we were Khatta's friends.

Was this another ruse? Or a real chance to come face-to-face with Khatta?

We had no option but to wait and watch.

Two days later, as directed, we reached the dhaba off the highway at Palwal. The owner seemed to be expecting us. He began chatting with us and when we asked about Khatta, he told us that Khatta knew of our arrival. Sure enough, our phone rang soon after.

'*Aap dono ko main dekh sakta hun. Main aas paas hi hun aur aapse jald aa kar milta hun.*' (I can see both of you. I am nearby and will come soon to meet you.)

We were feeling apprehensive by now. Could this be a trap? We had been 'seen'—identified—without having seen Khatta. We were clearly at a disadvantageous position. What if Khatta had reconciled with Gurmeet Ram Rahim? We felt exposed and vulnerable.

With all these doubts running through our minds, and our hearts thumping wildly, we were in a quandary. We decided to stay on and wait for Khatta.

The minutes dragged on. Half an hour passed, but it felt like several hours. Suddenly, our phone rang. It was Khatta. He hurriedly cancelled the meeting. 'It is not safe,' was all he had to offer as explanation.

This was becoming increasingly frustrating. We felt like we were being played. I sent a message to both his numbers saying that he either needed to trust us or let us know that he had no intention of speaking to us. We had had enough.

We called Shammy to tell her how Khatta continued to play hide-and-seek with us. Shammy, a veteran of many investigations, told us not to give up. She said it was important to keep pursuing him because it was entirely possible that Khatta was trying to gauge our seriousness. Also, he had major trust issues.

We returned to Sirsa and decided that it was finally time to head back to Delhi. Even as we were planning our return, all around us, Sirsa was turning into a fortress. The Dera chief had gotten embroiled in a major controversy that had nothing to do with the rape and murder charges that we were investigating. The Sikh community was at loggerheads with Dera Sacha Sauda after an advertisement was printed showing Gurmeet Ram Rahim Singh allegedly dressed up like Guru Gobind Singh, the tenth guru of the Sikhs.

In the advertisement, which appeared in local dailies in Punjab and Haryana and some national dailies on 14 May 2007, the Dera chief appeared wearing a *dumala* (round turban) with a *kalgi* (egret feather) and a *kamar kassa* (waistband)—very similar to the attire associated with Guru Gobind Singh. In the picture, Gurmeet was seen churning a huge vessel filled with milk with a serving spoon. The caption stated that Gurmeet Ram Rahim was making *Jaam-e-Insaan*—the elixir of humanity—or *roohani jaam*.

The picture had been taken during a religious congregation at Salabatpura village in Bathinda district of Punjab. It was a part of an advertisement by the Dera Sacha Sauda lauding the tenets of the sect.

Ironically, it was not the murders of Chhatrapati or Ranjit Singh, or the anonymous letter that carried explicit accusations of rape, that brought the Dera chief to the notice of the national media for the first time.

The advertisement sparked widespread protests by the Sikh community in Punjab, Haryana and parts of Rajasthan and Jammu. The Akal Takht, the highest temporal seat in Sikhism, called for a boycott of Dera Sacha Sauda, which would soon turn into a demand for the closure of all branches of the Dera across the country.

The first direct clash between the Sikhs and the Dera followers was reported from Sunam in Sangrur district of Punjab on 17 May 2007. Large numbers of Sikhs gathered near the Sunam Dera and went on a rampage, damaging shops nearby. The residence of the local Dera head was also allegedly attacked, but he escaped unhurt. This led to retaliation by followers camping inside the Dera at Sunam, as a result of which a Sikh, Kanwaljit Singh, was killed and fifteen people, which included followers from both sides, were grievously injured before the police could bring the situation under control.

The death of a Sikh at Sunam worsened the situation. As news of Kanwaljit Singh's demise spread, Sikhs started gathering in large numbers outside Dera Sacha Sauda branches across Punjab and Haryana.

More than twenty thousand Sikhs laid siege to the Dera at Salabatpura in Bathinda, the biggest Dera campus in Punjab. At the time, there were more than three thousand followers inside the Dera. This was happening even as other clashes were being reported from many parts of Punjab and Haryana. By the evening of 17 May, more than twenty-five people had been injured, while several vehicles and shops had reportedly been set on fire.

At the Talwandi Sabo gurdwara in Bathinda, one of the five sacred *takht*s (seats of authority) of Sikhism, tempers were running quite high. The news of the death of Kanwaljit Singh had reached the gurdwara. It was here that five high priests, under the chairmanship of the Jathedar of the Akal Takht, Joginder Singh Vedanti, finalized a five-point '*hukumnama*' (edict) against the Dera Sacha Sauda. The edict included the social boycott of the Dera and the registration of a police case against the sect for hurting the sentiments of the Sikh community. The Sikh high priests gave the Government of Punjab the deadline of 20 May to comply with their edict, failing which it would be 'forced to act against the Dera'.

We later learnt that most of the Sikhs attending this meeting were armed with weapons, mostly swords. Most people at the meeting wanted to act with immediate effect. When the edict was read out to them, many started raising slogans against the decision. We were told that one of the followers of the Damdami Taksal even threw a sword at Vedanti when he tried to leave the stage, which narrowly missed its target.

While the Sikhs were bracing themselves for clashes with the Dera followers, Gurmeet Ram Rahim himself showed no signs of relenting under pressure. The same day that the hukumnama was passed against him, the Dera chief held a meeting of his closest confidants at his headquarters in Sirsa. It was decided that they would condemn the attacks on the Dera followers in Punjab and Haryana. The Dera went on the offensive the same night, and its spokesperson, a bespectacled ophthalmologist, Aditya Insan, issued a statement saying that if the attacks on the Dera and its followers were not halted, the Dera's supporters could not be kept in check. Retaliation was on the cards.

With the situation spiralling rapidly out of control, and sensing imminent bloody clashes, the then Punjab chief minister Parkash Singh Badal convened an emergency meeting and requested the central government to deploy fifty companies of paramilitary forces in the state.

Acting on the request and sensing the gravity of the situation, the Centre rushed paramilitary forces to Punjab and to the Dera headquarters in Sirsa. In Punjab, where the situation had reached boiling point, more than forty companies of paramilitary forces and roughly one lakh Punjab Police personnel were deployed. Meanwhile, Sirsa had turned into a fortified town by the morning of 18 May 2007. A flag march was conducted to reinforce the presence of troops and to instil a sense of security among the common people.

The same day, reports of attacks on Dera properties started to pour in, especially from Punjab. Sangrur was completely closed down following the death of Kanwaljit

Singh. The Sikhs forcibly closed shops in the industrial town of Ludhiana, while effigies of the Dera chief were burnt in Sangrur, Jalandhar and Firozpur. The news started getting traction in the national media on 18 May, after Prime Minister Manmohan Singh issued a statement, saying, 'I appeal to the people of Punjab and Haryana to maintain calm. The situation should not be allowed to go out of control.'

This was when the national media rushed to Sirsa. Outdoor broadcast (OB) vans and camera crews with print and electronic media reporters seemed to carpet-bomb the city. Sitting in our hotel room, we spotted some familiar faces from our fraternity doing 'lives' from Sirsa. We called a few of them and learnt that the Dera's public relations (PR) machinery was in full swing. Media persons from Delhi covering the situation in Sirsa were getting calls from the Dera's PR, offering them stays at a resort near the Dera's new headquarters. We came to know that some journalists had already availed that offer.

With Khatta still evading us and Sirsa under lockdown, we thought it best to cover this latest controversy. Talwandi Sabo in Bathinda, from where the five-point hukumnama had been issued, was our first stop. During the 70–km drive from Sirsa, we witnessed an eerie silence. Most of the highway dhabas were closed, and barring some local vehicles, the normally busy highway was devoid of vehicular movement.

With a population of 20,589 people, mostly Sikhs, Talwandi Sabo is sanctified land for the Sikhs, being one of the five takhts of Sikhism and housing the Takht Sri Damdama Sahib, one of the most revered gurdwaras of the religion. Even before we could enter its city limits, all we could see around us were camouflage-attired men and heavy armoured vehicles.

In the city, we witnessed what seemed like a sea of Sikhs gathered at various points, many of whom were brandishing swords. The atmosphere was charged and this became even more evident once we entered the Takht Sri Damdama Sahib. Everywhere, we could hear people talking about Dera Sacha Sauda. Some of those whom we managed to speak to were unforgiving when the name of Gurmeet Ram Rahim was mentioned. 'He wants to challenge Sikhism. He thinks that he is God. Earlier, when Sikhs joined Dera Sacha Sauda, they were not asked to change their religion. But now, after he has taken over, he is forcing them to convert,' were some of the charges we heard.

We also managed to speak to one of the sevadars of the gurdwara and asked him about a possible clash with the Dera if the edict issued by the Sikh high priests was not followed. He was very clear that in such an eventuality, the Sikhs in Punjab and Haryana were ready to bring down the Deras in these two states. Surprisingly, among all the people we interacted with, only a handful were aware of the charges of rape and murder against the Dera chief. Their anger was almost wholly against a man daring to portray a likeness of their Guru. It was a clear indication that by and large, Dera Sacha Sauda had managed to contain news of other allegations against its chief.

After having langar at the gurdwara, we headed back to Sirsa. We ran into some of our journalist friends who were staying at the Dera's guest house in Sirsa. A journalist working for a national Hindi news channel, who was availing Dera Sacha Sauda's hospitality, told us that there was no sense of panic among the Dera followers. 'They are armed and ready to face any eventuality,' he told us. He gathered this information after speaking to some management committee members of the Dera. 'The baba has a huge support base. His men are trained in these kinds of combat.'

As the deadline of 20 May approached, there were reports of sporadic clashes, primarily in Punjab. Sirsa's borders were sealed and vehicular movement was restricted. Sticking to its defiant stand, on 19 May, the Dera spokesperson issued a statement that the Dera Sacha Sauda expressed regret over 'the chain of events' that had led to violence in Punjab, and that its head never intended to imitate Guru Gobind Singh. However, no apology was issued, which further added fuel to the fire.

Considering the backlash from the Sikh community, the Punjab Police registered a case against Gurmeet Ram Rahim on 20 May for inciting sectarian violence. He was charged under Section 295-A of the IPC (Indian Penal Code), relating to a deliberate and malicious act intended to outrage the religious feelings of any class by insulting its religion or religious beliefs. However, the Sikhs were not pacified.

At the end of the three-day deadline set for an apology, the five high priests met at the Golden Temple in Amritsar.

After a two-hour meeting, a fresh hukumnama was issued by the Akal Takht Jathedar, Joginder Singh Vedanti, which called for a statewide bandh in Punjab on 22 May. The state government was given a deadline of 27 May to close down all branches of the Dera.

Meanwhile, a delegation led by Swami Agnivesh, the social worker and Arya Samaj leader, reached Sirsa. The objective of this delegation was to broker a truce between the Sikhs and the Dera followers. It held meetings with the Dera committee members for two consecutive days, at the end of which, Swami Agnivesh announced that he had obtained a written apology from the Dera chief. However, a Dera spokesperson was quick to say that no such apology letter had been issued by Gurmeet Ram Rahim. The situation remained as it was.

On 22 May, as per the second hukumnama, the entire state of Punjab shut down. Businesses remained closed and public transport stayed off the roads. The situation was by and large peaceful. Reports from neighbouring Haryana were more worrying. Skirmishes between the police and Sikh protestors were reported from two places in Ambala, resulting in ten people, including one superintendent of police, being seriously injured. Reports of Sikh protestors burning effigies of the Dera chief came in from various places in Jammu and Kashmir too. Sirsa, however, remained peaceful, with security forces manning what seemed like every nook and cranny of the city. The journalists staying at the Dera guest houses would tell us that the Dera management remained unperturbed by these developments and it was business as usual. There was still no sign of the Dera chief tendering an apology.

From 22 to 27 May, the rumour mills worked overtime. Not a single day passed when we didn't hear false reports about the Sikhs marching from parts of Haryana and Punjab to lay siege to the Dera headquarters.

During this time, we met a veteran journalist, Harjeet Singh, who used to work for a local daily in Haryana. We asked him about something that had been perplexing all of us—why did the Dera chief not tender an apology and move on?

'This is a case of asserting power,' he told us. 'The Dera chief knows that if he apologizes right now, he will appear to have been defeated in front of his followers.' He told us that with the CBI after him, Gurmeet Ram Rahim wanted to make a forceful statement about the kind of clout he wielded among his followers. It was also a statement that Dera Sacha Sauda could challenge the Sikh community in their own stronghold. In other words, the Dera and its chief were not to be taken lightly.

Perhaps he was right. The deadline of 27 May was approaching and the state machinery of Punjab was under tremendous pressure from the Sikh community. Chief Minister Parkash Singh Badal was accused by the Akal Takht of being hand in glove with the Dera chief. His prestige was at stake, even as the Dera chief continued to be incommunicado, as he had been during the entire flare-up.

The deadline of 27 May finally arrived. Police and paramilitary forces were on high alert. At around noon, journalists started getting calls from the Dera headquarters in Sirsa and a press conference was convened in the late afternoon at the Dera guest house, where many journalists were staying.

The Dera spokesperson read out a statement: 'The Dera has already expressed regret for the chain of events and now, in the best interest of peace and tranquillity, the Dera tenders an apology to Guru Gobind Singh. Guruji [Gurmeet Ram Rahim] says that he never imitated or replicated the tenth Sikh Guru Gobind Singh.'

The statement further said: 'We also pray for maintaining peace and brotherhood in Punjab, Haryana, within the country and abroad.' It added that the Dera chief and his followers worked only for the unification of humanity. 'Guruji is a humble servant of humanity.'

With this statement, the press conference came to an end. No questions were asked or answered. The fine point was that nowhere had Dera Sacha Sauda apologized to the Sikh community and its highest temporal seat. The statement also managed to project its chief as someone who believed in equality and in uniting humanity.

The ball was now in the court of the Sikh high priests. The general notion was that Dera Sacha Sauda had cleared its stand and now the Sikhs would have to relent. The five Jathedars of the five takhts announced that they would meet on 31 May to decide whether to accept the apology or not.

Meanwhile, with this statement from the Dera, the tension began to, by and large, ease in both the states.

Media crews from New Delhi stationed in Sirsa started to pack up. We learnt that as a parting gift from Dera Sacha Sauda, many of them received expensive briefcases with 'gifts' inside. Is it any wonder, then, that if you assess media reports from that period, especially from the electronic media, in most of them Gurmeet was projected as the head of a sect whose sole purpose was to preach the religion of humanity? You would rarely find a report which mentioned that that wasn't his first brush with controversy, or reports that took any note of the fact that the man was accused of two murders and was being investigated for rape. If the reports that emerged in the national media were any indication, Dera Sacha Sauda had handled its first major encounter with the mainstream media quite well.

Though this controversy helped the Dera dig in its heels and assert its power in Punjab and Haryana, it would also come back to haunt the Dera chief from time to time. The sect, which was till then a minor irritant for the Sikhs, had become an eyesore, and in the months and years to come, the Dera followers and Sikhs would often face off over matters both big and small.

While a deceptive peace returned to Sirsa, it was time for us to get back to our original task—tracking our own version of the invisible man. The month of May was over and we were still looking for the one source that could help us decisively unmask the Dera chief.

'Kanta Nikaalo'

At around 9 p.m. on 1 July, I received a call from Khatta Singh. He sounded desperate and insisted that he wanted to meet us face-to-face. Past experiences had taught us to be wary of his assurances. I was sceptical, but then had no option but to say yes to him. I did tell him that it was becoming difficult for us to convince our superiors that he really did want to talk to us. As expected, Khatta was apologetic. There were 'security issues', he said, but now he had some friends accompanying him day and night. As a result, he felt safer than before.

A meeting was fixed for 3 July in Chandigarh. This time, I told him that we would choose the place. After all, he had seen us, but we hadn't seen him. And, given his multiple flip-flops, we were concerned about our own security.

To my surprise, he agreed. '*Is baar pakka mulakat hogi* (This time we will meet for sure),' he said as he disconnected the call.

I immediately called Ethmad and we decided to leave for Chandigarh early the next morning. We could only hope that Khatta wouldn't ditch us this time.

On reaching Chandigarh, we immediately started looking for a hotel that was in a crowded place, and which had an easy escape route. We found such a hotel in Sector 35 of the city. On either side, it was flanked by other hotels. All their roofs were interconnected. We were shown two rooms on the first floor. One of them had a window overlooking a green patch of ground. Ethmad immediately said that was the room we wanted. Later, when I asked him why, he said matter-of-factly, 'If Khatta double-crosses us, we can jump out of the window, land on soft grass and run away. Chances of injuries would be minimal.'

We couldn't help but laugh at our own fears, but then, we were dealing with someone who could possibly be acting on behalf of the Dera chief. We were yet to ascertain his authenticity as a source *against* Gurmeet Ram Rahim. Later in the evening, we climbed up to the terrace of the hotel and were relieved to see that it was connected to the terraces of adjoining hotels, with low boundaries on either side. We went to the terrace of the hotel next door and used its emergency exit to come out to the main road without anyone spotting us. This was our crucial plan B—exiting our hotel in case of an emergency.

With our plans laid out rather neatly in our minds and our questions framed, we checked and rechecked our recording equipment. The night was spent tossing and turning in anxiety.

The next day, at around 6 p.m., Khatta called us and asked us our location. 'I will be there in an hour,' he said. By 6.30, we were wired up and had double-checked our lights and other arrangements. The window facing the green patch was open, with its curtains drawn, our first emergency exit. The planner camera was tested for an angle against the chair on which we planned to have Khatta sit.

We then went up to the hotel's terrace, primarily to spot Khatta before he entered the hotel and also to look for any telltale signs of suspicious activity.

At around 7 p.m., Khatta called us and said that he was standing on the road in front of the hotel and asked for our room number. Indeed, we noticed a man wearing a blue turban and surrounded by burly men, talking on his phone while looking towards the hotel. I knew I was tempting fate when I told him that we wanted to meet him alone.

'*Aap mujhe kahan se dekh rahe hain?* (Where are you watching me from?)' Khatta Singh asked us. We told him that we were also worried about our security, and our experience with him so far had not been very good. All the time, we were keeping a watch on the man in the blue turban.

'*Achha, main in logon ko yahi rok deta hun, aur upar akela aata hun.* (OK, I will ask these people to stay here and will come to your room alone),' he said.

Immediately, we noticed the man in the blue turban gesture to the men with him to stay there while he walked towards the hotel. We finally had a face to the name. We told him the number of our room, whose door we had left open. *'Aap seedhe andar aa jayiega, room khula hai.'* (You can come in directly, the room is open.)

We then slipped from the terrace to the corridor of the first floor and hid ourselves near the emergency exit. The idea was to let Khatta enter the room and close the door behind him. The moment we saw him walking down the first floor corridor, we switched on all three of our cameras. Khatta went inside the room. We followed him into the room and bolted the door as per our plan.

Khatta was startled to find the door close behind him. He was ready to bolt. We tried to calm him down and said he could search us if he wanted to, even though we were wired. Fortunately, he said there was no need. We ushered him to the chair facing the planner camera.

During our initial conversation, we learnt that he joined the Dera in 1970. He told us that his parents were wealthy farmers from Chor Mar village in Sirsa, where they had forty acres of land. Later, the family sold it to move to Begu village near the Dera headquarters.

Khatta's parents had been *premi*s (disciples) of Dera Sacha Sauda since the time of Shah Mastana. He began visiting the Dera as a child with them. After formally joining the Dera, he would drop in every morning and evening because of his home's proximity to the campus. That was how he came in contact with Gurmeet Ram Rahim. In 1996, he was assigned the duty of driving the bus in which Gurmeet travelled. Later, he graduated to driving the Dera chief around in his fleet of luxury cars.

The stage was now set, the cameras were rolling. It was time to start asking the tough questions.

Tehelka: *Aap par koi direct attack bhee hua hai?* (Have
you ever been attacked?)
Khatta: *Abhi tak to na main kisi se daba hun ya dara
hun . . . Jitne din raha hun apne dum par hun.* (So far,
I have not feared anyone . . . I am alive because of my
own courage.)

He seemed to have settled down now. We felt we could get
to the real questions.

Tehelka: *Ranjit ko inhone kyon marwaya?* (Why did
they get Ranjit murdered?)
Khatta: *Woh to wahi hai ki uski behen ke saath bhee
balatkar kiya tha . . . Suman ke saath . . . Jab pata
chala Ranjit ko, tab usne (Gurmeet Ram Rahim) socha
ki Ranjit case wagairah karega Dere par, to yeh baat
thi ki Ranjit ko bata diya tha uski behen nein . . .* (His
sister was also raped and she had told Ranjit about it.
Gurmeet Ram Rahim thought that Ranjit might file a
case against the Dera.)

Khatta Singh claimed to have known Ranjit since 1990.
Because of his amiable disposition, Ranjit was universally
liked. When Khatta came to know that Ranjit was leaving
the Dera along with his sister and daughters, he asked him
why he was doing so. Ranjit was very dejected, Khatta
remembers, and he said, *'Mera Dere se bharosa uth gaya
hai.'* (I don't believe in the Dera any more.) This came as
a bit of a shock for Khatta, who knew that Ranjit was an
ardent follower.

Khatta asked around some more, and reached out to friends who were part of the inner circle around Gurmeet Ram Rahim. From them, he came to know that Ranjit's sister had been raped and this had shattered Ranjit. Meanwhile, he also came to know that Gurmeet and his men were using all forms of persuasion, including threats, to get Ranjit to return to the Dera.

> Tehelka: *Baba ko Ranjit se itna dar kyon tha?* (Why did the baba fear Ranjit so much?)
>
> Khatta: *Uss samay tak behen ki shaadi nahi hui thi . . . Uski doctri jaanch karwa di gayi to kya hoga . . .* (Ranjit's sister was not married at that time and they feared what would happen if she were medically examined.)

In the midst of all this, the anonymous letter surfaced in May 2002. Khatta told us that there was a sense of panic inside the Dera. Many veteran sadhvis were confined to what sounded to us like some sort of a torture chamber for days at a time, to find out who wrote the letter. Gurmeet Ram Rahim assigned the Dera manager, Krishan Lal, Inder Sain and Avtar Singh the task of tracing the writer of the letter. It was during this period that many local journalists were threatened and many others beaten up merely on the suspicion of having something to do with the letter.

Khatta said, '*In logon nein baba ko bataya ki Ranjit nein hi letter likha hain . . . Phir kuch dinon baad Ranjit ko Dera bulaya.*' (These people told Gurmeet that the letter was written by Ranjit. After some days, Ranjit was summoned to the Dera.)

When Ranjit came to the Dera on 16 May 2002, Khatta said he saw him and rushed up to him.

> Tehelka: *Ranjit ki aapse kya baat hui?* (What did you talk about with Ranjit?)
> Khatta: *Usne bola ki baba Gurmeet nein use bulaya hai. Woh kaafi dara hua tha.* (He said that he had been called by Gurmeet. He was very scared.)

While he was talking to Ranjit, Avtar Singh, Inder Sain, Krishan Lal and one Darshan Singh came up to Ranjit and seemed to be forcing him to confess in front of the Dera chief that he had written the anonymous letter.

Khatta said, '*Woh usse baar baar baba se maafi maangne ke liye dabav bana rahe the.*' (They were constantly putting pressure on him to tender an apology to the Dera chief.)

According to him, Ranjit was adamant and maintained that neither had he written the letter, nor would he seek forgiveness from anyone. To that, one of Gurmeet's men said, '*To phir marne ke liye tayyar raho.*' (Then get ready to die.)

These men then forced him inside the gufa, where Gurmeet asked him to come back to the Dera and work there like he used to. Ranjit refused, saying that it was not possible any more for him. He then left the Dera.

> Tehelka: *Phir kya hua?* (Then what happened?)
> Khatta: *Ranjit jab bina maafi maange Dere se chala gaya to baba nein ussi shaam gufa mein ek meeting bulai.* (After Ranjit left the Dera without apologizing, Gurmeet called a meeting inside the gufa that evening.)

Avtar Singh, Inder Sain, Krishan Lal, Jasbir Singh, Sabdil Singh (Gurmeet Ram Rahim's gunman) and Darshan Singh were at that meeting. Khatta claimed to have also been present.

Khatta said, *'Baba Gurmeet bahut gusse mein tha.'* (Gurmeet was very angry.) He ordered his men to go to Ranjit's village and kill him before he spilt the beans.

Khatta continued, *'Yeh kuch bole isse pehle iska kanta nikaalo.'* (Before he says anything, get him eliminated.)

(Khatta clarified that 'kanta nikaalo', which literally means 'pull out the thorn', was the code used by the Dera chief to order someone to be killed.)

Khatta said he learnt about Ranjit Singh's murder on the evening of 10 July 2002, the very day he was killed. Even as he was dealing with his own grief, he saw Avtar Singh, Jasbir Singh, Sabdil Singh and Krishan Lal celebrating Ranjit's death at Hotel Kailash, which is located on the road opposite the new Dera.

Khatta said, *'Main jab unke paas gaya to unko kehte suna ki gaddar ko maar diya.'* (I overheard them saying that a traitor has been eliminated.)

He corroborated most of the information we already had about Ranjit's murder. He also confessed to having witnessed the conspiracy being hatched inside the cave to murder Ranjit.

We asked Khatta about the murder of Ram Chander Chhatrapati.

Tehelka: *Chhatrapati ke saath kya hua tha?* (What happened with Chhatrapati?)

Khatta: *Uska murder bhee isi baba nein karaya jab usne apne akhbaar mein woh letter chhaap diya.* (Gurmeet got him murdered after he published that letter in his paper.)

He said that a day before Chhatrapati was murdered, on 23 October 2002, he had published a long piece in *Poora Sach* about the sexual exploitation of sadhvis, in which he spoke extensively about Gurmeet Ram Rahim. That morning, Khatta drove Gurmeet to Jalandhar in his Land Cruiser.

'Ham chhe baje shaam wapas Sirsa pahunche, jahan Krishan Lal nein baba ko woh paper dikhaya.' (We returned to Sirsa at 6 p.m., where Krishan Lal showed the paper to Gurmeet.)

Khatta said that apart from him, Gurmeet and Krishan Lal, two other Dera premis were present in the gufa— Kuldeep Singh and Nirmal Singh. On seeing the paper, Gurmeet flew into a rage and asked Krishan Lal, Nirmal and Kuldeep to shut Chhatrapati's mouth forever.

Khatta said, *'Yeh sunne ke baad Krishan Lal gufa se bahar gaya aur thodi der baad walkie-talkie ka set lekar andar aaya. Usne apni revolver inko di saath mein walkie-talkie bhee.'* (After listening to this, Krishan Lal went out of the cave and returned with a walkie-talkie set. He also handed them his revolver.)

Krishan Lal asked them to execute the murder as ordered by Gurmeet Ram Rahim, while instructing them to keep him informed via walkie-talkie.

Khatta claimed to have left the next day for Delhi for personal work.

'*Raat mein mujhe mere ghar se phone aaya ki kisi nein Chhatrapati ko maar diya hain aur police nein Kuldeep Singh ko pakad liya hain.*' (I got a call at night from my home informing me that someone had killed Chhatrapati and the police had arrested Kuldeep Singh.)

He was surprised, he said, that Kuldeep Singh and Nirmal Singh had acted on the Dera chief's orders so swiftly.

Tehelka: *Aapke saamne do hatyaon ka plan banaya gaya, magar aap police ya CBI ke paas kyon nahi gaye?* (Two conspiracies of murder were hatched in front of you. Why didn't you approach the police or the CBI?)

Khatta: *Mujhe apne pariwaar ki chinta thi . . . jisne bhee baba ke khilaaf bola use isne marwaa diya.* (I was worried about my family. Whoever said anything against the baba, he had them murdered.)

Gurmeet's henchmen had made him sign on many blank sheets of paper, he said, and he was worried that these might be used to trap him.

Next, we asked him about Fakir Chand, who, according to police records thus far, remained 'missing'. '*Aapne Fakir Chand ka naam suna hain? Uske saath kya hua?*' (Have you heard the name of Fakir Chand? What happened to him?)

For once, Khatta seemed to be taken aback. He became nervous and, staring at the planner in front of him, suspiciously asked, '*Aap kahin mujhe record to nahi kar rahe ho?*' (Are you recording my statement?)

His question made us nervous in turn. Keeping calm was the urgent need of the moment. We told him that if he wanted to leave, he was free to do so. It was a chance we took. I asked him where he thought the cameras were. 'Check the diary if you want to,' I said, with my heart in my mouth. All he needed to do to blow our cover was open the planner.

To our great relief, he said there was no need to do that. Ethmad was simply staring at me. I could get his unspoken message, 'I can't believe what a fool you are.'

But it was a risk that paid off. It gave Khatta the encouragement he perhaps needed to start sharing information about the alleged murder of Fakir Chand.

'*Fakir Chand jo tha woh Shah Satnam baba ka bahut khaas tha. Uske paas Dere ka sara hisaab-kitaab rehta tha. Is baba ko woh bilkul pasand nahi karta tha, yeh baat Dere mein sabko pata thi.*' (Fakir Chand was a close confidant of the previous Dera chief, Shah Satnam. He used to keep all the accounts of the Dera. He didn't like this baba. Everyone at the Dera knew this.)

Khatta said that once Gurmeet took over as the Dera chief, he wanted Fakir Chand to give him all the details about the wealth the Dera had accumulated over the years. When Fakir Chand refused to do so, saying that the money was strictly for the welfare of the Dera premis, he was taken to the torture room and imprisoned there for a few days. He was given no food and was beaten up from time to time. Those 'taking care' of Fakir Chand included a former driver, Gobind Singh, Baldev Singh Bahedi, Sukhdev Singh Bawana and a sadhvi, Resham.

Fakir Chand was shifted to a farmhouse about 7 km away, on the road leading to Phoolkan village. Here too, he was beaten up and further interrogated. Once he divulged the details, the plan was to murder him in three days' time. But Fakir Chand sustained a fatal injury while being tortured at the farmhouse and died. According to Khatta, on the directions of the Dera chief, the accused burnt the hair off Fakir Chand's dead body and threw it into a canal near the farmhouse.

This revelation established two things. First, it corroborated Ram Kumar Bisnoi's belief that Fakir Chand had been murdered. Second, it established the crime scene.

Ranjit's and Chhatrapati's were the two murders that the CBI was probing. Fakir Chand was not even on their radar.

Little did we know that Khatta was about to tell us about another murder, which perhaps no one outside the Dera, and very few inside it, were aware of.

Tehelka: *Aur kiska kiska murder karwaaya hai baba nein?* (Who else has the baba gotten murdered?)

Khatta: *Murder to ji bahut saare karwaye hain, jaise ek Lakshaman Das ka.* (He has had many people murdered, for instance, Lakshaman Das.)

Tehelka: *Lakshaman Das kaun tha?* (Who was Lakshaman Das?)

Khatta: *Woh purane baba ka khana banata tha.* (He used to cook for the previous Dera chief.)

Khatta claimed that Lakshaman Das was murdered because he refused to acknowledge Gurmeet Ram Rahim's authority. A rumour was spread that he had committed suicide by consuming poison because he was mentally disturbed.

This was growing beyond our wildest imaginations, but then, we had one serious practical issue at hand. The camera's recorders, which were in our front pockets, were getting heated up. It was impossible to sit without fidgeting and it was also equally important to ensure that it had not gotten overheated and stopped recording.

As planned earlier, Ethmad excused himself to use the washroom. The idea was that at least two cameras should be functional when one was given a break. There remained one on the buttonhole of my shirt and the other on the planner. Ethmad came out of the washroom after two minutes. After bearing the heat for another minute, I excused myself as well. To my delight, the camera was still recording. I switched off the recorder for a minute or two, and then switched it back on. It was working perfectly. Which was just as well, since Khatta was moving ahead at full tilt and no longer needed any prompting.

He next told us about a room in the new Dera premises where sadhvis who refused to go to the gufa or who tried to escape the Dera were confined and tortured. A sadhvi from Bathinda had fractured her spine when she was beaten up mercilessly by Gurmeet's henchmen. Apparently, the sadhvi had been called to the gufa and raped by Gurmeet Ram Rahim. When she went back to the girls' hostel, she was in extreme pain and confided in another sadhvi. Unfortunately, said Khatta, the sadhvi she confided in was one of the many moles Gurmeet had planted inside the girls' hostel.

Next day, the sadhvi was summoned to the torture chamber and brutally beaten with belts and canes by four men. When she was dragged out of the room, she was bleeding profusely and Khatta later learnt that her spine had been badly damaged. Her parents were summoned to the Dera and the sadhvi was handed over to them.

> Tehelka: *Phir kya hua uss sadhvi ka?* (What happened to that sadhvi?)
> Khatta: *Baba apne aadmi bhejta raha Bathinda . . . woh uske mata–pita ko lagatar samjhate the ki baat bahar na aaye.* (Baba would regularly send his men to Bathinda to tell her parents that word about this should not get out.)
> Tehelka: *Kya sadhvi wapas aayi Dera par?* (Did she come back to the Dera?)
> Khatta: *Uski to reed ki haddi toot gayi, baba ke kisi kaam ki nahi thi. Usko samjha-samjhu ke wahi mamla daba diya.* (Her spine was broken. She was of no use to the baba any more. So he got the matter settled.)

Not only the sadhvis but the sadhus too, if they rebelled against the Dera chief's authority, or were found saying anything against him, would be subjected to the same treatment. It was difficult to keep anything from Gurmeet because of his spy system. Khatta said that for every four disciples, one would be selected to snitch on the other three. No one knew who these spies were who would report to the baba's henchmen. There was a general sense of distrust among the disciples and this was the reason why despite their sufferings, they would keep everything to themselves.

Khatta said, *'Dera mein kaun apna hain kaun paraya, pata karna bahut mushkil ka kaam tha.'* (It was very difficult to find out whom you could trust and whom you couldn't at the Dera.) He said that the penalty for speaking against either Dera Sacha Sauda or its chief was severe. The price of rebellion was torture, if you were lucky, and murder if you weren't. In some cases, if a sadhu wanted to leave the Dera, he was allowed to. He would be followed by the Dera's henchmen and a few miles away, scores would be settled. In some cases, he claimed the deserter was beaten up, and in some cases, he was simply murdered.

Tehelka: *Yeh kaise hota tha?* (How was this carried out?)
Khatta: *Bas ji speed se aakar uske upar gaddi chada dete the. Mamla accident ka bata kar nipta dete the.* (They would hit him with a speeding vehicle, and then make it look like an accident and settle the case.)

For every kind of criminal activity, the Dera chief had devised a system of code words. The meanings of these code words were known only to ten to fifteen close confidants. For instance, the person assigned to summon a sadhvi to the gufa would say she had been called for 'Pitaji ki maafi' (Father's forgiveness). The sadhvis all knew that if a particular sadhvi had been given 'maafi by Pitaji', she had been through the same horror they had been subjected to earlier. 'Kanta nikaal dena' (remove the thorn) was the code used when the Dera chief had decided that someone needed to be murdered, probably because he had become a 'thorn' in his side, like what happened with Ranjit Singh. When a murder was executed by mowing down someone, usually a deserter, with a vehicle, the code used was *isse farmhouse bhej diya'* (he has been sent to the farmhouse).

Khatta said that while driving the Dera chief, whenever he heard the words *'isse farmhouse bhej diya'*, he would shiver at the thought that one more person had been murdered.

When asked why the sadhvis did not try harder to escape the Dera or expose their exploitation by the Dera chief, Khatta grew pensive. *'Iska itna mayajaal faila hai Dera premiyon mein ki maa–baap bhee apni ladkiyon ki nahi sunte.'* (He has created such an aura around himself that even parents don't listen to their daughters.)

He told us about a seventeen-year-old sadhvi who managed to scale the wall of the girls' hostel and escape the Dera. When she reached home and told her parents about the Dera chief molesting her, her parents refused to believe her. *'Uske maa–baap nein bola ki TV, picture dekhne ko nahi milta hoga isliye tu bhag aayi hain. Tera hi character kharab hoga. Pitaji kuch galat nahi kar sakte.'* (Her parents told her that she had probably escaped from the Dera as she was not allowed to watch TV and movies there. She must have done something wrong. Pitaji can't do anything bad.)

The very next day, her parents brought her back to the Dera and handed her over to Gurmeet.

Tehelka: *Phir uss ladki ke saath kya hua?* (Then what happened to that girl?)

Khatta: *Hona kya tha? Usko torture room mein kai dino tak bhookha–pyasa rakha. Baba ki ek khaas sadhvi usko roz maarti thi.* (What do you think happened? The girl was kept in the torture room for several days without any food or water. A sadhvi close to the baba would beat her every day.)

In the course of our conversation with Khatta, we learnt about an orphanage run by the Dera near its campus. He alleged that the baba had not spared girls as young as twelve or thirteen. *'Main daawa karta hun ki is anathalaya ki bacchio ka medical kara lo, sab sach saamne aa jayega.'* (I'm sure that if a medical test of these girls is conducted, the truth will come out.)

Even as we were taking in the extent of sexual exploitation perpetrated at the Dera, Khatta drifted on to a different topic, something we were hearing for the first time in the course of our investigation.

'Kabhi fanki ka naam suna hain?' (Have you heard of 'fanki'?)

We were nonplussed. Fanki?

'Fanki afeem ka waste hota hai. Baba us fanki ko subah bhandaare ki rotiyon mein milwa deta hai aur uske baad saare Dera premi usi nashe mein kaam karte hain. Jab nasha halka

padta hai to dopahar ke khaane mein bhee wahi milaya jaata hain. Isliye log baba ke paas solah-solah ghante bina kuch shikayat kare kaam karte hain.' (Fanki is a residue of opium. The Dera chief has it mixed in the rotis served during the community breakfast. All the followers go about their day under its influence. When by afternoon, the high wears off, fanki is again mixed into the food served for lunch. This is the reason people work at the Dera for sixteen hours without complaining.)

We then asked, *'Yeh fanki baba ko kaha se milti hain?'* (Where does the baba get this fanki from?)

Khatta replied, *'Rajasthan ke Malwa ilaake mein baba ke lakhon premi hain aur Dere ki bahut saari jameen bhee. Wahin iss afeem ki kheti hoti hai.'* (In the Malwa region of Rajasthan, Gurmeet has lakhs of followers, and the Dera owns vast tracts of land in that region. It is there that this opium is produced.)

When we tried to probe further into the source and production of opium under the Dera's tutelage, Khatta said that its production was something he was not very sure of.

Khatta was about to reveal another use of fanki at the Dera, which turned out to be yet another example of Gurmeet's depravity.

'Sadhuon ko napunsak banane ke liye bhee baba fanki ka istemaal kartá hai.' (Gurmeet also uses fanki during the castration of sadhus.)

We probed further: *'Yeh to ekdum nayi baat hai. Yeh kaise hota tha?'* (This is something new to us. How was this done?)

Khatta proceeded to make a shocking revelation. He told us that Gurmeet had till then castrated more than three hundred sadhus living at the Dera. Some had left and a few had been murdered. He told us about a boy who was killed after he protested his castration at the Dera. He was once a close aide of Gurmeet, and the Dera chief feared that he might leave the Dera and expose him.

According to Khatta, Gurmeet castrated followers close to him to ensure their loyalty. The castrations, according to Khatta, were conducted at a 400-bed super-speciality hospital owned by the Dera in Sirsa.

'Jis din kisi ko napunsak banana hota hai, use subah se afeem ka nasha karwaya jaata hai jisse woh sunn pad jaaye aur ussey koi dard na ho aur woh virodh bhee na kar paaye.' (The day someone is to be castrated, he is made to take opium from the morning onwards so that he feels no pain and is unable to resist when being operated on.)

For this purpose, Gurmeet had appointed two surgeons, who were also his disciples.

This was something we needed time to digest. However, time was running out and we needed a few more details from Khatta while he was still in the mood to talk.

Tehelka: *Yeh gufa ka kya mamla hai?* (What is this cave all about?)
Khatta: *Gufa woh jagah hai jahan baba apne saare kale kaarnamon ko karta hai.* (The gufa is the place where the baba does all his evil deeds.)

Khatta corroborated the sadhvi's story of the two gufas. He said that the old and the new Dera campuses had their own separate gufas. In the old Dera, the gufa was directly connected to the girl's hostel. At its gate, sadhvis were on duty day and night. A sadhvi called Sheila Punia assigned sadhvis to sentry duty at the gate of the gufa at the old Dera, he said.

Talking about the gufa at the new Dera, he said, '*Aap jaisa soch sakte ho waise saari suvidhayen hain uske andar.*' (Whatever luxury you can think of is available in the new Dera's cave.)

The entire length of its corridor was illuminated by psychedelic lights to give the impression that one was entering a different world. Air conditioners ran on full blast to maintain a sort of surreal Himalayan atmosphere, while projectors flashed images of Gurmeet Ram Rahim.

Khatta: *Bade-bade mukhya mantri aur mantri ki frame kari hui photo lagi hui, gallery se lekar baba ke main kamre tak. In photuon mein yeh neta baba ke pair chhoote hue aur ashirwad lete hue dikhte hain.* (Framed photos of chief ministers and ministers adorn the entire gallery right up to Gurmeet's chamber, in which these people are seen touching Gurmeet's feet and seeking his blessings.)

Tehelka: *Kaun kaun se neta aate hain baba ke pas?* (Which political leaders come to visit the baba?)

Khatta: *Chahe Parkash Singh Badal ho ya Congress aur BJP ka koi bada neta, sab baba ki ek phone call par maujood rehte.* (Whether Parkash Singh Badal or any other leader from the Congress or the BJP, they are available to the baba at one phone call's notice.)

Khatta said that Gurmeet's alleged proximity to political leaders was one of the reasons that people were scared to speak up against him.

In another major disclosure, Khatta told us how Gurmeet had taken over the reins of the Dera from Shah Satnam in 1990.

'Iska ek dost tha . . . shayad rishtedaar. Uska naam tha Gurjant Singh Rajasthani. Ek din Gurmeet apne dost Gurjant aur uske kuch saathiyon ke saath Baba Satnam ke paas pahuncha. Gurjant nein baba ki kanpati par AK-47 laga ke Gurmeet ko Dera mukhiya banane ke liye kaha.' (He had a friend . . . perhaps a relative. His name was Gurjant Singh Rajasthani. One day, Gurmeet came to the Dera along with Gurjant and some of his friends. Gurjant pointed an AK-47 at Shah Satnam's temple and asked him to appoint Gurmeet the Dera chief.)

Within a few days of this incident, that is exactly what Shah Satnam did.

An hour had passed since Khatta came to the room and started talking. The recorders were heated up and we feared that the battery would give up any time. Khatta's phone too began ringing incessantly. He told us he needed to leave. Once he was out of the room, we switched off the cameras, collected our equipment and backpacks, locked the room and ran up to the terrace. We saw Khatta leave in a Bolero jeep.

We agreed that we needed to get out of the hotel immediately. We rushed to the reception right away, where we made the excuse of a medical emergency and hurriedly paid our bills. Soon, we were out on the road.

We knew that there was a good chance that someone was following Khatta and, in turn, had gotten on to our trail as well. Our hearts were thumping. Danger seemed just around the corner.

Within a few minutes, we spotted a state roadways bus. Clueless about its destination, we boarded it. By the time the conductor came to us for tickets, we had covered a few kilometres. We told him it seemed we had boarded the wrong bus. He was kind enough not to ask us any further questions. He asked us to get down at a dhaba. With the passing moments, our anxiety quietened somewhat.

After having a calming cup of tea, we called Shammy.

'Operation Jhootha Sauda accomplished!'

'Congratulations! Hope you guys are safe. Come back to Delhi at the earliest,' she said.

We decided to get some sleep at the dhaba. A major part of the operation was complete. Now, it was finally time to show the world the real face of Gurmeet Ram Rahim Singh.

Part II

From Dera to Empire

The Backstory

On the afternoon of 31 August 1991, the public announcement system installed in the Dera headquarters in Sirsa, old and new, came to life. The Dera premis were asked to maintain absolute silence that day following the announcement. It was a direct order from the Dera chief, so no one dared ask why they had been asked to do so. This ritual was repeated for three consecutive years, on the same day, and then discontinued.

In the wee hours of 31 August 1991, in Phase 7 of Mohali, a company of the Punjab Police had surrounded house no. 127. Holed up inside the house was a dreaded terrorist with a reward of Rs 20 lakh on his head. His name was Gurjant Singh Rajasthani, and he was the self-proclaimed chief general of the Khalistan Commando Force. Gurjant was wanted for hundreds of murders in Punjab, Haryana and Rajasthan. After a fierce gun battle, he was shot while trying to escape.

You might wonder what connects the two events mentioned above, apart from the fact that they occurred on the same day.

Gurjant Singh and Gurmeet Singh were born in the same village—Sri Gurusar Modia—in Ganganagar district of Rajasthan. Both belonged to affluent landowning families in the area. Gurmeet's father, Maghar Singh, a Jat Sikh by caste, was a well-known landlord. Both the boys had little or no interest in studies and discontinued going to school after completing their basic education.

Maghar Singh was a staunch disciple of Shah Satnam and was active in spreading his teachings. Acknowledging the fact that his son had no interest in formal education and was possibly drifting towards antisocial activities, Maghar Singh made sure that Gurmeet accompanied him every time he visited Shah Satnam. Though unwillingly, and after some initial resistance, Gurmeet gave in to the demands of his father and started visiting the Dera.

Meanwhile, in a property dispute, an uncle of Gurjant was murdered in the village. Hot-blooded Gurjant vowed revenge for the murder and, within a few days, killed his uncle's murderer. He was arrested and jailed, which was where he was radicalized by separatist Khalistani militants. When he was released, Gurjant joined the Khalistan Commando Force. His rise through its ranks was considered phenomenal.

Gurjant and Gurmeet remained friends. It was a friendship that would prove to be beneficial to them both. But before we get to that, let's briefly understand the history of Dera Sacha Sauda and why it succeeded in garnering the support of millions across Punjab, Haryana, Rajasthan and other parts of North India.

As the Dera's website and other records available online show, an ascetic, Mastana Balochistani, born in the Baloch region of south-west Asia, who was a follower of one Baba Sawan Singh, arrived in Sirsa in 1948. On 29 April that year, he established Dera Sacha Sauda (literally, the camp of those who have made a deal with the truth).

Caste, religion and age were no bar in joining the Dera—a radical concept for the times. Balochistani laid down three principal tenets for those who wished to join the Dera: no consumption of meat or eggs, no consumption of drugs, tobacco or alcohol, and no adultery or illicit sex. He devised a meditation method that he named 'Naam', and coined the Dera chant—'Dhan Dhan Satguru, Tera Hi Aasara'.

After the establishment of the first Dera in 1948, within a span of fifteen years, he succeeded in opening twenty-five centres across Punjab, Haryana and Rajasthan. 'It was his simplicity and his teachings that attracted people towards him,' said a septuagenarian Dera premi, Ratan Singh, while remembering Balochistani. Ratan, who lives in Begu village in Sirsa, said that he joined the Dera when he was just fifteen. At the time, the greatest emphasis was on how to become a better human being. 'There was complete parity among followers. You could be from any economical background, any caste or religion; once you were a Dera premi, everyone was equal,' he said.

In 1963, the reins of the Dera were handed over to Shah Satnam by Mastana Balochistani. It was under his regime that the Dera expanded the most in terms of followers. Besides sticking to the principles of his predecessor, Shah Satnam started expanding the Dera's methods of generating revenue to community farming and community meals. Many of those who joined the Dera in this period sold their ancestral lands in their native villages and purchased land near the villages surrounding Sirsa. Landless Dalits who were working as farm labourers on landholdings belonging to upper-caste Sikhs soon started joining the sect, though initially in small numbers.

'They felt safe, secure and equal. They were given an equal share of the farm earnings. Earlier, they worked in the farms of landlords for a pittance with no dignity of their own,' Ratan said, explaining the reason for the drift of the Dalits towards the Dera.

What Ratan said is endorsed by several scholars who have worked on caste politics in Punjab and Haryana. As a political scientist from Punjab University, Ashutosh Kumar, told *Frontline* in 2009:

Dalits espoused Sikhism in the beginning for three main reasons: first, Sikhism didn't believe in the caste system; secondly, it allowed everyone to wear arms, which was perceived as a matter of pride; and thirdly and most importantly, it glorified manual labour, unlike Hinduism. But in reality, the caste system still prevails, leading to disillusionment among the Dalits. Perhaps it is this contradiction between the perceived and the actual that is making the Dalits drift towards the deras.

Under Shah Satnam, Dera Sacha Sauda provided what Dalits were looking for—primarily a non-sectarian space, in contrast to both the Hindu and Sikh religions. They were looking for the basic minimum respect that they were deprived of, and the Dera gave them that and more—land to plough and an equal share in its produce. The discrimination of Dalits at gurdwaras, led by upper-caste Jat Sikhs, was another major reason for the Dalits to join the Dera. It may be interesting to note that as per the census in 2011, Punjab, with 32 per cent scheduled castes, is the state with the highest Dalit population in the country. And a large majority of them were working under a feudal system and living under discriminatory conditions. The emergence of the Dera was a welcome escape from oppression.

The Dera also invested in skill training for its followers to make them self-sufficient. It started packaging farm produce and selling it in the open market at competitive rates. The Dera's economy began to show signs of robustness not only because of this but because of a generous amount of funds it received from expatriate Dalit Sikhs who wanted to see their community prosper in the land they had left behind.

Gurmeet Singh, who was whiling away his time at the Dera's headquarters in Sirsa at his father's insistence, and was doing odd jobs like driving a tractor and helping organize langars, was witness to the Dera's economic growth.

'He showed little interest in the teachings of the sect. He showed more interest in its management,' was the view of a former disciple of the Dera who had left when Gurmeet took over. He said that Gurmeet was not remarkable, as was falsely projected in the Dera's promotional literature. 'He regularly boasted of his connection with strongmen outside the Dera,' the former disciple said. Apparently, Gurmeet was even reprimanded by Shah Satnam for his behaviour with other Dera followers. So, for a majority of them, it came as a shock when, in September 1990, Shah Satnam, in a surprise public announcement, appointed Gurmeet as his successor and gave him the name 'Huzoor Maharaj Gurmeet Ram Rahim'.

Many former Dera followers say that when Shah Satnam had announced his plans for retirement earlier that year, he had zeroed in on three contenders. Gurmeet's name was nowhere close to that list. However, at the age of twenty-three, in September 1990, Gurmeet Singh was elevated to the position of the spiritual head of the influential Dera in what seemed like a miracle.

Some say it was a pistol, some say it was an AK-47—the weapon of choice in the separatist militancy that thrived in Punjab through the 1980s—that caused the miracle.

By 1990, the Punjab Police was rooting out the last traces of militancy in the state. Gurjant Singh Rajasthani knew that the Dera had enough clout to prevent the police from swooping down on it whenever it wanted to. Also, its premises could be used for two more purposes—hiding weapons, and routing money from the offshore accounts of the overseas supporters of the Khalistan movement.

According to an unverified theory, Gurjant and Gurmeet hatched a plan. Shah Satnam had already announced his retirement and it was merely a matter of time before he announced his successor. They had to act swiftly. In the third week of September, late one night, Gurmeet facilitated Gurjant's entry, along with his accomplices, into the Dera and led them to Shah Satnam's quarters. The old and fragile Dera chief was woken up by armed men who asked him in no uncertain terms to name Gurmeet as his successor. The announcement was made within a few days of this alleged incident.

During our investigation, we found that after Gurmeet took over, Gurjant asked him to construct secret bunkers within the Dera premises to store weapons. Also, from December 1990 to August 1991, when he was killed, Gurjant used the Dera's accounts to route offshore funds from Khalistan supporters. Gurmeet was not complaining—the unaccounted-for money and the new power afforded by sophisticated weapons made him feel more powerful and in control than he had ever before, a high he would seemingly get addicted to.

It was a personal loss for Gurmeet when Gurjant was killed on 31 August 1991. So distraught was he when the news reached him that he ordered the observation of complete silence at the Dera. Gurjant's passing also meant that the unaccounted-for money and weapons stashed at the Dera had no claimant. Other than Gurmeet.

Unlike the first two Dera chiefs, Gurmeet's philosophy was far from spiritual. It was oriented from the beginning towards the acquisition and accumulation of power. To this end, he clearly understood the importance of having the clout that would come with vast numbers of followers.

One of the first things on his agenda was to acquire as much land as he could around the two Dera campuses—legally or illegally. His former associate divulged that he wanted to build his own empire where he would be king and have his private army, his own currency, his own laws, and so on. When Gurmeet took over in 1990, the Dera owned some five acres of land on record. By 2017, his empire in Sirsa would extend to more than 700 acres of land, excluding many unaccounted-for 'benami' (unnamed) properties belonging to the Dera.

In order to fund his grandiose plans, the Dera chief began manipulating the minds of his followers. He started telling them that if they desired to connect directly with the Supreme Power, they had to show a willingness to give away their worldly possessions to the Dera, including donating their lands. Many who fell prey to this blindly signed sales deeds in favour of the Dera at throwaway rates. The Dera, in turn, sold these lands at a premium and used the money to buy more land in Sirsa.

Farmers who had land adjoining the Dera's in villages like Shahpur Begu, Khaja Khera, Phoolkan, Kanganpur, Bajekan, Ali Mohammad, Nejia, Arniyanwali and others were first asked to sell their land as per the price fixed by the Dera. Many farmers willingly sold their land to the Dera. One of the reasons was that the influx of Dera followers in the area had become a nuisance for the local population and many wanted to relocate. Those who refused were arm-twisted into submission.

'We were asked to cut the barbed wire of an adjoining farm at night. After that we let animals loose, which trampled on the standing crop. This went on for days,' explained a former associate of the Dera. The harassed farmer would complain to the police. With the local police on the payroll of the Dera, it was the farmer who was reprimanded for making false allegations against the Dera. After being harassed mentally and economically in this way, the farmer would eventually give in and sell his land to the Dera at dirt-cheap rates.

In some cases, indirect intimidation was employed. Goons would gather in large numbers around the land to be acquired and camp there for several days. They would beat and abuse some random Dera follower mercilessly in front of the farmer to instil fear in him. This method too worked.

But the way that worked best to coerce people to sell their land was a brainchild of the Dera chief. He would organize congregations just a few paces away from the land he wished to acquire. Lakhs of followers would be asked to attend the congregation. They would then be asked to dump all the garbage that would accumulate on each day of the congregation on the said piece of land, and use it for defecation.

Within a week, the piece of land would turn into a garbage dump. The locals feared raising their voice before such a huge gathering, and those who resisted would often be roughed up. Eventually, the farmer who owned the land would be contacted and offered a deal by the Dera, which, in most cases, he would accept.

These lands, acquired from farmers at throwaway prices, would, in turn, be leased at premium rates to followers who wished to settle with their families near the Dera premises. The hefty profit was pocketed by the Dera, and the land and its owner also became part of the Dera.

In early 2000, its land-grabbing got an impetus, with the Dera acquiring greater muscle power in Punjab, Haryana and Rajasthan.

The beginning of the agrarian crisis in Punjab and Haryana—both beneficiaries of the Green Revolution at one time—resulted in the slowing down of the economies of these states. With Sikh landlords diversifying into other businesses, the landless Dalits felt further marginalized as their wages dipped. This resulted in further friction between the landed and the landless. Looking for cheap labour, landowners in these states started employing labourers from Uttar Pradesh and Bihar. The Dalit farm workers were left to fend for themselves.

Simultaneously, there occurred a huge surge in the Dera's following, with Dalits turning to the sect in large numbers to escape further deprivation and marginalization. The Dera following grew manifold, with the youth forming a major portion of it. Most of them sought land to work on and a sect of their own where they were treated as equals.

As his wealth grew, Gurmeet knew he was close to realizing his dream of building his own empire. To protect it, he knew he would need a private army.

In early 2000, the Dera chief discussed the idea with some Indian Army veterans who were Dera followers. A blueprint was made and recruitment for the purpose began.

The recruitment procedure for the Dera's private army was loosely based on the process followed by the Indian Army. A jawan, once recruited, underwent rigorous physical training under the supervision of ex-army men. They were trained in the handling of small arms and other weapons.

The Dera's militia had three wings. The inner wing was to closely guard Gurmeet, and was hand-picked by the trainers. This wing's responsibility was to steer the chief away from the site during an eventuality.

The second wing was to provide external cover while the Dera chief was shifted to a safe base in case of a crisis. The outer wing was to monitor every corner of the Dera premises and not let anyone in during a crisis.

The ex-army men trained hand-picked followers in military tactics, such as the usage of petrol bombs. A war room equipped with CCTV cameras was built in both the old and new Dera campuses, and private army members were given walkie-talkies to communicate with.

It may be noted that in 2010, through its intelligence network, the Indian Army got a whiff of the fact that some ex-army men were imparting weapons' training to the Dera followers. In an internal letter dated 13 December 2010, signed by Lt Col N.S. Bhatti, it was stated that 'some ex-service men are engaging themselves in imparting weapon training to activists of Dera Sacha Sauda at their HQ located in Sirsa'. The letter further stated that 'reportedly, some serving personnel have been participating in activities of Dera Sacha Sauda, like blood donation camps'. The letter instructed that the directive to stay away from Dera Sacha Sauda should be intimated to everyone at unit and subunit levels for strict compliance.

One wing that the Dera chief, with the help of his ex-army followers, had been gradually building since early 2000, and which would prove to be the Dera's most dreaded force, was one that perhaps no other religious sect in India had ever thought of. It was called the Qurbani Dasta (Sacrifice Wing).

In effect, the Qurbani Dasta was not very different from suicide bombers in any terrorist organization— completely radicalized and ready to die or kill, spill blood on the streets, all at a single command from the Dera chief.

The first time the existence of this wing was noted was on 2 July 2007, when a Dera follower, Jaswant Singh, in broad daylight, poured kerosene on his clothes and set himself ablaze in front of the Sirsa District Court. He was protesting the registration of the case against Gurmeet Ram Rahim for attempting to impersonate Guru Gobind Singh. While immolating himself, he was shouting, *'Mere jaise lakho hain jo babaji ke liye marne maarne ko tayyaar hain.'* (Like me, there are lakhs who are ready to die or kill for Gurmeet Singh.) He was close to a spot where twenty-five other Dera followers were observing a hunger strike. With 80 per cent burns, Jaswant was rushed to the government hospital where, a few weeks later, he succumbed to his injuries. The local intelligence later learnt that Jaswant was part of the Qurbani Dasta raised by Dera Sacha Sauda.

The second time the Qurbani Dasta's existence was noticed was in September 2017, after Gurmeet Ram Rahim was convicted in two rape cases by a CBI court. The wing reportedly issued threatening letters to journalists, Haryana Police officers, former Dera followers, and witnesses who deposed against Gurmeet Singh. The letter was sent to several media houses that covered the proceedings of Gurmeet's conviction and carried reports of his misdeeds. The letter said that 200 youths were ready to sacrifice their lives for Gurmeet. In a chilling reminder of the Dera's tactics of threats and intimidation, the letter went on to say that this band was looking for the family members of those maligning the Dera chief and would kill them systematically.

'We are already like living corpses, but now we will kill those who have been making false propaganda against the Dera along with their family members,' the letter said. Its heading was, *'Teesri Adalat Ka Faisala Sazaye Maut'* (Death Sentence by the Third Court).

A journalist friend with whom I had worked in 2003, and who had shifted to Chandigarh almost ten years ago, helped fix up a meeting with a former follower who had been selected for the Qurbani Dasta but who later ran away from the Dera as he was not ready to either die or kill. The meeting was held in Greater Noida, where he lived in a one-room apartment while working at a factory manufacturing auto parts.

'I moved to Greater Noida in 2008, immediately after I left the Dera. I had studied some basic mechanical stuff at the Dera and it helped me get a job here,' he said, a medium-built man in his mid-thirties. 'I am happy that finally that monster is in jail; I wish he never comes out of it now.'

He said he used to live in Phoolkan village in Sirsa district. He was just eight when he lost his father, an alcoholic, to liver cirrhosis. His mother died a year later. At the age of nine, he was sent to the Dera by his relatives. It was around the time when Gurmeet took over the Dera. He remembers the first few years as being fairly decent. 'We were encouraged to study in the school within the Dera premises. Orphans were given special care, with Dera followers providing us with clothes, books and stationery. It was quite a disciplined life,' he recalls.

Things started changing for him in 2004, when he was summoned by Gurmeet to his gufa. 'It was very unusual for a regular Dera follower to be called by baba inside the gufa. I was nervous.'

Once he entered the gufa, he saw Gurmeet standing with two Dera premis who were popularly called 'Faujis'. No one knew their real names. Gurmeet told him that he was a divine soul who had been chosen for a special purpose. To fulfil it, henceforth he must only speak to and listen to the Faujis. He would not be staying in the orphanage hall any more and would be provided special accommodation.

Indeed, he was shifted to rooms located on the outer periphery of the Dera, abutting dense vegetation. There, he met more than three hundred other young men of his age. 'We were handed a schedule that outlined a daily regime with specific timings for waking up, running, physical exercise, spiritual training, and so on.'

At 4.30 a.m. sharp, they were woken up and after a glass of milk and a banana, were made to run 5 to 6 km. After a short break, they were given physical combat training. 'In the afternoon, we had long spiritual classes where most of the time, the emphasis was on the fact that life is ephemeral and we were born for a higher purpose,' he recalled. 'Our minds were conditioned to give up all worldly things and think of death as the ultimate sacrifice.'

After basic training, they graduated to training in batches, supervised by the Faujis, to handle small arms like revolvers and automatic pistols. They were trained to assemble petrol bombs, how to create a panic in a large crowd and get away without being noticed. He said that, like him, most of the others had no idea why this kind of training was being imparted to them. To help them catch up on their studies, teachers would come to them—they were not allowed to go to the school and mingle with their old friends.

'This was all very suspicious and scary, but no one opened their mouth,' he said. During his stay at this camp, he learnt that most of the other participants were either orphans like him or had been abandoned by their parents and were at the mercy of the Dera. He learnt another secret that shocked him to the core—that some of the boys had been castrated.

'One fine day, the Faujis brought us sweets and new clothes and announced that we were now ready to be part of a divine team,' he said. 'They said that we were the elite members of the Dera's Qurbani Dasta, one of the most revered and feared wings of the Dera, which was willing to die or kill for the chief.' He was stunned. 'All my life, I hadn't even killed a bird. Killing a man was beyond my imagination. It felt so repulsive. I wanted to run away from the Dera then and there.'

Unlike him, most of the boys welcomed their new-found status. They were all then allowed to resume their normal life at the Dera with the express instruction not to divulge a single detail of their training to anyone and to keep the identity of their wing secret. They were told that they would be called for assignments as and when required.

He continued with his studies and also learnt basic mechanics at a skill training centre at the Dera. In June 2007, he heard about Jaswant Singh's self-immolation. 'Jaswant Singh was trained along with us. Now my only wish was to escape the Dera at the earliest possible opportunity.'

In 2008, he was assigned to go to Sirsa city to bring spare parts for vehicles used within the Dera. 'I was handed the cash. It was enough for me to escape Sirsa,' he said. Once in the city, he boarded a bus to Delhi. Someone on the bus told him that there were factories in Greater Noida where he could get a mechanical job, and that was how he landed up here.

In 2009, he contacted my journalist friend after he saw him do a show on Gurmeet on a national TV channel. 'I got his number through the channel's Chandigarh bureau. I told him a few details. He asked me whether I would speak on record. But I feared that if I did so, I would be killed.' Since then, he had kept in touch with him and when he called after Gurmeet's arrest, he was more than willing to share the details while hiding his identity.

'All these years, I lived in perpetual fear of being killed. Now that he is behind bars and the Dera is almost dismantled, I can live a normal life,' he said, tears welling up in his eyes.

Years of living in fear is not something I would wish for anyone. I left him with a prayer in my heart that his scars may one day be healed. But there were scores of other Dera followers whose lives would never be the same again, even after Gurmeet's conviction.

'Mujh Par Rehmat Ho Gayi'

As you approach house no. 323 in ward no. 11 of the Tohana Bazigar area of Tohana, in Fatehgarh district of Haryana, you can hear music wafting out. The soft strains of a mandolin play in the background to accompany voices of children singing bhajans in unison. One can't help but stop for a while outside, just to listen to the music. The nondescript house has a small signboard that says 'HS Academy'.

After savouring the music for a few moments, I rang the bell. A man who seemed to be in his late forties opened the gate. I told him that I had an appointment with the music teacher. I was ushered into a room where the music teacher, in his mid-thirties, appeared completely lost in singing, his fingers plucking at the mandolin. There were five students in the room who repeated after him. I sat quietly, not wishing to interrupt the class, while enjoying every single note emerging from the group before me.

While the bhajan was in Punjabi, and it was difficult for me to make out the exact meaning of the words, there was something so soulful about it that one could not help feel stirred.

Time seemed to glide past. It was impossible to make out from the face of the teacher, lost in the world of music, all that he had gone through and continued to. Today, I was to meet Hansraj Chauhan, a former Dera sadhu, who had been subjected to castration in 2000.

In another half hour, the class came to an end. 'You have a soulful voice. I was lost in the song and your music,' I complimented Hansraj. He smiled and said, 'This is all I am left with. My life hinges solely on music.'

I had first met Hansraj in 2012. In the five years since, his appearance had changed considerably. He seemed to have put on a lot of weight and had little trace of facial hair. 'It's all the effect of castration. The body is thrown out of balance. The hormones are completely unbalanced, which has had an impact on me,' he said, perhaps sensing my gaze on him.

Hansraj's family were Bazigars, a scheduled caste, and barely managed to make ends meet when they joined the Dera in the early 1970s. Hansraj became a follower at a very young age. During his teenage years, he remembers once being assigned to do *seva* (service) in Kota, Rajasthan. 'Kota was flooded because of the overflowing Chambal River. The lives of the Dera premis camping in Kota was in danger. I was a good swimmer and managed to save the lives of seven premis,' he recalls.

His courage was much talked about among the Dera followers and reached the ears of Gurmeet Singh. 'Baba praised me and presented me with a bouquet of flowers.' Since 1990, Hansraj had been working as a sevadar in the Dera canteen at Kota. In 1995, Gurmeet Singh went to his house to meet his parents. He told them that their son had extraordinary courage and devotion and that he wanted to take him to Sirsa and make him a saint. The family, though staunch followers of the Dera, were not ready to give away their son. 'I was preparing for my class ten examination. My family wanted me to continue with my studies. My parents were very reluctant initially.' However, Gurmeet's close aides continued to visit their house to convince his parents. 'Your son has been hand-picked by the chief himself. He was born for a higher spiritual purpose,' was their argument.

After a few months of being coaxed and cajoled in this manner, his parents gave in and agreed. In January 1996, Hansraj moved to the Dera headquarters in Sirsa.

The same year, in the presence of his family and a few other sadhus of the Dera, Gurmeet Ram Rahim formally ordained him as a sadhu after administering two pieces of sweet to him. He was assigned to be a part of the Shahi Bhajan Mandali.

With his natural flair for music, Hansraj soon became a popular bhajan singer at the Dera. He started strumming a guitar and with regular practice, became good at playing it. Soon, Hansraj was made the head of sound system management at the Dera.

'In 1999, some other sadhus and I came to know of an experiment of castration on a horse at the Dera. The animal died after three months.' Hansraj said this was the first time he had heard about castration. He heard that the chief had decided to conduct the same experiment on humans. Initially, a member of the senior management staff known to be close to Gurmeet was made to undergo the operation. In late 1999, the chief called a meeting of 500 sadhus at the Dera headquarters. These sadhus were part of Dera Sacha Sauda's Saint Brahmachari Sevadar group.

During that meeting, the sadhus were told that they had to go through a minor surgery which would bring them 'directly in touch with God'. Gurmeet Ram Rahim explained that this surgery would take away all their worldly worries and bring them a step closer to heaven. The sadhus were then introduced to two doctors— Dr Pankaj Garg and Dr M.P. Singh. Gurmeet said that these two doctors were trained in the 'special surgery' and added that it would be painless.

After the meeting, Gurmeet met the sadhus one-on-one. 'Those who agreed to go through the surgery at that time did not exactly know what it was all about. They were treated royally that day,' Hansraj recalls. Those who refused to comply were humiliated and abused by Gurmeet. Some were even sent to the torture room and beaten up for days.

To begin with, two sadhus, Ratan and Dharam Singh, who was also the personal cook for the Dera chief, underwent the surgery. Makeshift arrangements were made inside the gufa and the doctors mentioned by the Dera chief in the meeting conducted the surgery. Mohan Singh Diwana, Mittu Singh and Gurjant Singh, three close aides of Gurmeet, were the next ones on whom the surgery was performed.

These sadhus were strictly told not to reveal to other sadhus that they had been castrated. Gurmeet told them to propagate among others that after the surgery, they could see God and felt close to Him. They were to tell the other sadhus that the surgery had led their mind to a higher realm of spirituality and they could now communicate directly with the Supreme Power because of their enhanced powers of concentration. At the chief's directions, the castrated sadhus conducted meetings with eighteen to twenty young sadhus on a regular basis in an attempt to brainwash them and make them believe that the surgery would miraculously transform their lives.

In October 2000, Hansraj was travelling with Gurmeet Ram Rahim to his hometown in Gurusar Modia in Rajasthan. 'I was a bhajan singer, so Gurmeet used to take me along to his hometown every time he visited, to perform bhajans.'

On the way, Gurmeet told him, *'Tum par rehmat ho gayi hai'* (You have been blessed), and that soon, Hansraj would have a vision of God. 'Little did I know that this trip would ruin my entire life.' Hansraj was then seventeen years old, and completely unaware of the trap he was falling into.

Dera Sacha Sauda runs a hospital at Gurusar Modia, Gurmeet Singh's village in Sri Ganganagar district. According to Hansraj, most of the initial castrations were done at this hospital. He said that the Dera chief asked him to go to the hospital and meet Dr Garg and Dr Singh, and say to them, *'Mujh par rehmat ho gayi.'* (I have been blessed.)

When he went to the hospital that evening and told the doctors exactly what the Dera chief had asked him to, they smiled and offered him a cold drink. 'Even before I could finish half the bottle, my head started spinning and I began to hallucinate. Soon, I fell unconscious, to wake up three days later.'

His ordeal had only just begun.

On regaining consciousness, he found his private parts bandaged. 'I was in immense pain. I cried out and was given painkiller injections,' he said, recalling the horror. In the evening, when the dressing was changed, he realized that his testicles had been removed. 'Out of fear, dejection and pain, I urinated on the bed itself,' he said, tears welling in his eyes while recounting that day. He wanted to die. His belief in the Dera and its chief was shattered. He felt betrayed.

'Where to run away, whom to tell what has happened to me, how will I live the rest of my life—these were some of the questions running through my mind.'

He confronted the doctors who operated on him, only to be told that he was 'chosen'—he had been specially ordained by 'God' Gurmeet himself, and should have no reason to complain, nor should he tell anyone at the Dera.

'I refused to eat anything. I was just crying and thinking of my parents. After some time, I fell unconscious again.'

Even seventeen years after the surgery, Hansraj says that the pain refuses to go. 'Sometimes it hurts so much, it feels as if hundreds of scorpions are biting me at the same time.'

Hansraj was discharged from the hospital the next day and sent to Sirsa. There, many sadhus his age asked him the reason for his despondency, but he kept it to himself. There were two reasons for that—he feared for his life, but perhaps the greater one was that he felt ashamed. Soon after he returned, another sadhu his age was summoned by the Dera chief. *'Uspar bhee rehmat ho gayi.'* (He too was blessed.) That sadhu, also a minor, was sent to the same hospital in Gurusar Modia. 'When he came back, he was seething with pain. His operation seemed to have gone wrong and there were blood stains on his pyjamas.'

This pattern of selecting young boys and sending them to be castrated continued for a long time. Hansraj said that from his group alone, more than twenty minors were sent for the surgery. With the number of castration cases increasing in number, keeping it secret became difficult. Soon, most of the sadhus at the Dera became aware of it. Some tried to flee to avoid it. Those who were caught trying to escape were beaten up and put in the torture room for days.

The doctors were called from the Dera hospital in Rajasthan and a makeshift operation theatre was created in Sirsa where the sadhus were forcibly castrated. 'We used to hear screams emanating from the tent. Sadhus used to cry loudly and beg to be released. They would be sedated and operated upon. The castrated sadhus were kept in a state of trance throughout the day, either with opium or pills used for sedation.

'Every morning before breakfast, we were handed round black tablets that we were told were meant to suppress sexual desire. The impact of the pill was so intense that our minds would become numb. We were incapable of thinking after taking the tablet. We were in a perpetual state of trance.'

As per Hansraj's own estimate, more than two hundred sadhus had been castrated by the end of 2002. He mentioned two cases, one in which three brothers were castrated and another in which two brothers were castrated. 'Imagine the plight of those parents, all three of whose sons were castrated,' he said.

In 2002, a meeting of the castrated sadhus was convened by the Dera chief, in which he told them that for the outside world, they were 'eunuchs' now. They could neither marry nor procreate. They would soon start looking more like women than men, and if they left the Dera, society would not accept them. They should therefore pledge their complete allegiance to him, and give him complete control over their lives and deaths. Henceforth, they should do whatever assignment they were given without question, even if it involved dying or killing.

From the group, Gurmeet selected more than hundred sadhus and said they would constitute the core of his private militia. Many of these sadhus were inducted into the Qurbani Dasta as well, and were ready to commit suicide at the instructions of the Dera chief. Some were given the duty of guarding the gufa and moving around with Gurmeet as his personal bodyguards.

After the sadhus were provided training in handling small weapons, it was announced by the Dera chief that whoever wanted to buy a licensed pistol or revolver, its cost would be borne by the Dera. Many sadhus opted for it.

'I was offered a licensed pistol to conduct heinous crimes. Thankfully, I was educated enough to refuse. But the others weren't so lucky. They fell for it and were used to commit crimes on behalf of the Dera chief.'

Here, I will digress a bit from Hansraj's account and tell you about two incidents that reveal how the castrated sadhus were used by Gurmeet, and the extent to which they had been brainwashed.

On 23 March 2011, Gurmeet was called to the Sirsa court complex for questioning via videoconferencing, by the CBI court handling the rape and murder charges against him. After Gurmeet had left its premises, the court reverberated with the sound of a gunshot. A Dera follower, Vinod Kumar, was found to have shot himself through the temple inside a car parked in the court complex. The suicide note recovered from the victim stated that he was disturbed by the fact that Gurmeet had been unnecessarily dragged into controversy.

Within one month, on 28 April 2011, Gurmeet was again called for questioning via videoconferencing by the

CBI court, this time in connection with Ranjit's murder. The same pattern was followed. A forty-two-year-old Dera follower, Suraj Bhan, from Jind, shot himself in the stomach, again after the Dera chief had left the complex at around 3.30 p.m. The suicide note recovered from him more or less mirrored Vinod Kumar's. It said that he was upset about Gurmeet Ram Rahim's repeated appearances before the CBI court in criminal cases. Postmortem reports in both the cases found the victims' testicles missing. Clearly, this indicated that both were part of the Dera's Qurbani Dasta, and it can be concluded that they had been brainwashed to commit suicide so as to put pressure on the investigating agency and the judiciary.

It is also surprising to know that most of the accused in Chhatrapati's and Ranjit's murders, including Krishan Lal, the Dera manager, were castrated.

To come back to Hansraj, he told me that after his betrayal by the chief, he had lost all interest in the Dera's activities, though on the face of it, to avoid beatings or torture, he continued with his routine, singing bhajans in the Dera congregations. From time to time, he expressed to Gurmeet his desire to leave the Dera, saying that he missed his home and wanted to go back and live with his parents.

'Each time, Gurmeet Ram Rahim would respond by saying that there was no place left for me in the outside world and that people would not accept me.' The actual reason for not letting him go was possibly that the chief feared that once Hansraj, or any of the other castrated sadhus, left the Dera, they might talk about being castrated at the Dera. Whenever his parents visited the Dera, he thought of telling them. However, he feared that his parents might not be able to take the shock. 'They would ask me why I was not my usual self. Why I always appeared sad. But I kept my sorrows within me,' a teary Hansraj told me.

By October 2009, he was sick of the Dera. The hormonal changes that were a direct result of the castration were beginning to visibly impact his body. 'My breasts began to grow and my facial hair thinned and became scanty.' He thought that there might be a reverse surgery that might help him. This could only be possible outside the Dera. It was at this time that his parents came to visit him.

'That day was the toughest for me. I was about to reveal to my parents that I had been castrated.' As he told his parents about his ordeal, he couldn't stop crying. His parents were shell-shocked. They had no words with which to console him.

'I begged my father to save me and take me away from the Dera.'

Hansraj's parents spoke to Gurmeet Ram Rahim without revealing in any way that they knew of their son's condition. They requested him to allow Hansraj to leave the Dera. After several rounds of convincing, Hansraj was relieved from the Dera on 15 October 2009.

'I left everything I had at the Dera and reached Tohana in the kurta-pyjama I was wearing. My fourteen years of exile had finally come to an end.'

The initial days were very tough for the family. Hansraj's father tried to put on a brave face, but his mother was severely traumatized.

'For days in a row, my parents could not eat anything. I was holed up at home, too scared to go out and meet any of my childhood friends.' The Dera chief's men kept an eye on him for months. To alleviate any suspicion that he had cut all ties with the Dera, Hansraj continued to occasionally participate in the sect's congregations.

Despite his family's efforts to keep it under wraps, the news of his castration spread in the village. 'People, including kids, would taunt me and call me a eunuch. They used to clap, imitating the way eunuchs do it, and take digs at me.'

He said that he had lost all hope, but then something within him snapped.

'A friend of mine called me from Ghaziabad in 2010. He was also a Dera follower. He was distraught because his younger brother, who was twenty-three, had also been castrated at the Dera.'

Hansraj said that when he realized that castrations were still going on at the Dera and many more young men were likely to face the kind of suffering that he had, he decided to do something about it. He had come to know an old Dera friend and former sadhu, Gurdas Singh Toor, popularly known as 'Bittu'. Toor worked at the Dera's printing press and was close to some sadhus who were part of the Dera chief's inner circle. Toor claimed to have become disillusioned with

Gurmeet Ram Rahim after witnessing certain incidents related to the Dera chief's involvement in Ram Chander Chhatrapati's murder.

Once out of the Dera, Toor became actively involved in collecting evidence against Gurmeet and his henchmen. He came to know another former sadhu, Jatinder Singh, also known as 'Gora'. Gora too had left the Dera and was running a mobile phone shop in Sirsa city. He had also been castrated during his time at the Dera.

Toor, Gora and Hansraj secretly got together and started preparing a list of sadhus who had been castrated at the Dera. Gora, who was Net savvy, ensured that they established contact through the Internet. He also handed Toor a list of the names of 400 sadhus, which included his own name, who were castrated at the Dera.

Then Gora and Toor came to know about a youth from Malout who had gone missing under mysterious circumstances.

'While Toor and Gora would meet in Sirsa often, I would talk to them on the phone. The Dera henchmen did get a hint that something was cooking between Toor and Gora, but they were not aware that I too was a part of the group and that we were making a list,' Hansraj told me. Meanwhile, Hansraj was on the lookout for a lawyer who could advise them and file a formal criminal case against the Dera chief. He would closely follow reports in local newspapers about developments in the cases against the Dera chief. In one such report, he read the name of senior lawyer Navkiran Singh.

'Whether it was divine intervention or something else, the moment I read how relentlessly Navkiran Singh was following cases against the Dera, I decided to meet him.' He called Toor and expressed his desire to meet Navkiran Singh. They went together to meet the lawyer.

'When I started narrating what I had gone through at the Dera and told him about the castration of hundreds of other sadhus, it all seemed unbelievable to him,' Hansraj said, recalling his first meeting with the lawyer. Navkiran consoled him and promised to bring the case to its logical end. Moreover, he took the case on a pro bono basis. In the third week of July 2012, Hansraj filed a petition in the Punjab and Haryana High Court through his counsel, Navkiran Singh.

In the same month, something else happened that left Hansraj and Toor completely shaken. Their friend and ally, Jatinder Singh 'Gora', went missing on 6 July 2012. The man who could have been a prime witness in the castration case vanished into thin air.

During our investigation, we learnt that the Dera chief and his men had got wind of the fact that Toor and Gora were collecting evidence in the cases of castration and might approach the court soon. They had been in touch with many former sadhus who were willing to depose in court.

'I spoke to Gora a day before he went missing. We were all scared yet excited 'that finally, the truth was going to be revealed,' Hansraj said. Toor had his last contact with Gora on the day he went missing. They spoke over the phone. Hansraj later learnt from his sources at the Dera that the day Gora went missing from his home, he had been seen at the Dera.

'I was told that he was shot dead and his body burnt after kerosene was poured on it.'

Soon after, the news that Hansraj had filed a case against Gurmeet Ram Rahim for forcible castration became known. It was Hansraj's turn to be at the receiving end of the Dera's intimidation. 'Several motorcycles used to make the rounds of my house at all times of the day and night. Faces covered with cloth, they would shout threats and hurl abuses at me.' On the pretext of meeting his parents, many Dera premis started frequenting his house. From offering money to direct threats, every possible means was tried to persuade him not to pursue the case.

Hansraj had been trying to make a living by teaching at a local school, but was asked by the school's administration to quit. 'The Dera people pressured the school management, and they, in turn, had no option but to ask me to leave.'

In December 2014, the efforts of Navkiran Singh and Hansraj seemed to bear some fruit. The Punjab and Haryana High Court handed the case over to the CBI and asked the agency to interrogate Gurmeet Ram Rahim. While handing the case to the CBI, Justice K. Kannan made a strongly worded observation against the Haryana Police. He said that he had been forced to hand the case over to the CBI because the Haryana Police had run a 'worthless' investigation into the case, allowing 'grass to grow under its feet and nibbling at the periphery'.

In October 2017, the high court gave a final deadline to the CBI for completion of the probe into the castration charges against Gurmeet and his aides. The court asked the CBI to submit the charge sheet in the case by 1 February 2018. Buoyed by the success in nailing down Gurmeet in the rape cases, the CBI accelerated the pace in this case. And after Gurmeet was convicted in the rape case, many sadhus who were castrated but feared that they might be killed if they opened their mouths, started approaching the agency to narrate their ordeal. After recording the statement of scores of such sadhus, the CBI filed a charge sheet on these allegations against Gurmeet and two of his aides, Dr Pankaj Garg and Dr M.P. Singh. This charged Gurmeet and the doctors of criminal conspiracy, voluntarily causing hurt using dangerous weapon(s) and criminal intimidation, and was presented in the court of the special judicial magistrate of Panchkula.

Meanwhile, Hansraj's struggle with social stigma continues even today. His parents never recovered from the trauma. They were ostracized from their social circle. Many friends and relatives made it clear that they wanted nothing to do with the family because of the fear of a backlash from Dera Sacha Sauda.

'My parents never recovered. They stopped going out. They remained holed up in the house most of the time.' He lost them both in 2016. Since most nearby schools, on one pretext or another, refused him a stable job, he started teaching music at Bachpan International Public School, which was 20 km from his residence.

'All was going well, but after the verdict in the rape cases against Gurmeet Ram Rahim in August 2017, the school asked me to take a break.' Undoubtedly, it was to avoid being associated with someone who was also fighting against the Dera chief.

Hansraj is sure that one day, justice will be done. What worries him is, will society change its outlook towards him?

'Sometimes I feel it is much easier to fight this monster than brave the comments and taunts I am subjected to by society, including even people who were part of my childhood years. I am ready to give anything so that my life becomes what it was before castration. I am fighting two battles simultaneously. One is within my body, and the other is external, with the society and the stigma it attaches to people like me.'

Honeypreet and
the Travails of a Dera Family

When I contacted Vishwas Gupta, his response was, 'Yes, come and meet me any time. I don't have any work anyway. I don't step out of my home much as I am sick and tired of being taunted and identified as Honeypreet's ex-husband. My identity as an individual has been reduced to this.'

For the Indian media and for most of us, Honeypreet Insaan was an unknown entity till the Dera chief was arrested and convicted in two cases of rape of former sadhvis in August 2017. It was when a photograph surfaced showing Gurmeet Singh minutes after his conviction, seated in a fifteen-seater AgustaWestland helicopter with Honeypreet accompanying him, that she became a subject of media debate and salacious conjecture. The woman seen accompanying the convict was immediately identified as the Dera chief's 'adopted daughter'—her

Twitter handle proclaimed her to be 'Papa's favourite angel'. Speculation was rife in the media about whether she was likely to be Gurmeet Ram Rahim's successor as head of the Dera.

The thirty-six-year-old went missing on the day of Gurmeet Ram Rahim's conviction, after escorting the Dera chief on the chopper from Panchkula to a jail in Rohtak. Honeypreet was later arrested by the Haryana Police after being on the run for thirty-eight days and was charged for inciting the violence and rioting that followed the conviction, which left forty-one people dead and thousands injured. At the time of my meeting with Vishwas, Honeypreet was lodged at Ambala Central Jail.

Forty-year-old Vishwas's only condition prior to the meeting was that his father would be present too. His experience with the media after Honeypreet came into the limelight had been bitter. He alleged that whatever he said would, many times, be misconstrued and moulded by media persons as per their convenience. While we were setting up the meeting on the phone, he said that his father had been associated with Dera Sacha Sauda since 1970, had severed the association in 2011, and would be in a better position than him to explain the family's ordeal after Gurmeet Singh took over as the Dera chief.

Once I reached Karnal, Vishwas guided me over the phone to a society where his family was staying. While I was parking my car, I was greeted by a man who seemed to be in his early seventies. He identified himself as Vishwas Gupta's father and escorted me to a flat. 'This flat is used as a guest house by the society and this is where we meet the media. Vishwas has remarried after his divorce with Honeypreet and has a daughter who is a few months old. We don't want to put them under any kind of media scrutiny.'

Vishwas was already in the flat, flanked by security personnel from the Haryana Police. My first impression was of a man who had lost all interest in worldly life and was whiling away his time. On the table in front of where we were sitting was a thick file. 'It contains the documents pertaining to the long legal battle we fought against that rapist,' Vishwas's father M.P. Gupta said with obvious distaste.

After a brief silence, he started speaking about his life without any prompting. After studying civil engineering at a prestigious engineering college in Chandigarh, he found employment as an SDO (sub-divisional officer) in the Haryana irrigation department and was posted in Chandigarh. He was twenty-four years old at the time when a junior colleague introduced him to Dera Sacha Sauda.

'The junior engineer working under me was a Dera disciple. He told me that this was a miraculous cult whose head, Shah Satnam ji, was an incarnation of God.' The junior engineer told him about all the miracles he had witnessed and asked him to go and listen to the religious discourse given by Shah Satnam at the old Dera in Sirsa.

'After a lot of convincing on his part, I decided to go to the satsang in Sirsa. And that first impression of Shah

Satnam left an indelible impression on my mind.' He took the *naam* (formal joining of the sect) on the same day— 18 April 1970.

The conditions for joining the cult were very simple— stop eating non-vegetarian food, including eggs, avoid any kind of addiction or intoxication, and shun illicit relations or promiscuity.

'It was all very simple. The Dera was open to everyone, be they from any caste or religion. No money or alms were accepted by the Dera. During those days, there was not even a tea shop in the vicinity of the Dera,' Gupta recalls.

Gupta came from a wealthy and influential family in the Gharaunda constituency of Karnal district, from where his father had been elected twice as an independent MLA, from 1962 to 1968 and from 1972 to 1977. He said that he was so impressed by the sermons and teachings of his 'sant' that he convinced all his family members to join the cult. Gradually, he became close to Shah Satnam and started accompanying him wherever he travelled to deliver discourses.

In 1980, when Shah Satnam established a Dera in Barwana in Bagpat district of Uttar Pradesh, on the Baraut–Meerut road, he asked Gupta to take over its administration. 'It was not a full-time job. He trusted me to manage this new Dera, so I could not refuse.' He worked as its '*prabandhak*', or manager, for a considerable period. He also took a vow to become a sadhu with the Dera and remained one for thirteen years.

'My son was born in 1977. I used to travel with my wife and him along with Shah Satnam ji. He had a minimalistic approach to life and was devoid of any desire for worldly comfort.' Vishwas, who had been listening to our conversation, said, 'There were times when we would stay in huts in small villages where Satnam ji travelled for his discourse.'

Gupta said that all was going well till 1990. That was the year Shah Satnam handed over the reins of the cult to Gurmeet Singh. 'This is where I and several other followers of Shah Satnam ji made one of the biggest mistakes of our lives. We blindly accepted this rapist and murderer as the true successor of our guruji,' Gupta said with deep regret. Many old followers of Shah Satnam did leave, but people like him stayed loyal to the Dera. Gupta also refuted the theory that it was Gurjant Singh Rajasthani who was instrumental in installing Gurmeet Singh as the Dera chief. 'Shah Satnam ji was a real saint. He could never have been forced to do anything against his wishes.'

After Shah Satnam's death on 13 December 1991, for one year, Gurmeet did not step outside the Dera. He started conducting 'satsangs' within its premises and during the whole time, spoke little, instead asking devotees to share their experiences and the miracles they had witnessed during Shah Satnam's life. Devotees like Gupta would speak during these gatherings.

'It was a sinister ploy by Gurmeet. During these sermons, he made lists of people like us who were dedicated followers of the Dera and the previous guruji. He knew that it was devotees like us who would do anything for the Dera.' During this one-year period, Gurmeet also formed a fair idea of the financially well-off devotees and those who were strong and influential in various respects, and who could be called upon to render services to the Dera. He also made a recording of the 'divine' and miraculous experiences shared by the old devotees. These were converted into a religious book that was distributed as promotional material to influence greater numbers to join the sect.

Gurmeet knew about Gupta's financial standing and would often praise him in front of the congregation. He was accorded special treatment, like many other devotees who could part with their money for the Dera. Gupta said that initially, Gurmeet, on one pretext or another, would ask him and others to donate money for the Dera's expansion. For instance, one day he announced he would write a book of philosophy and it would be accorded the status of a *granth* (sacred text). He asked every devotee to deposit Rs 25,000 for this purpose.

'People like us were so blind that crores of rupees were collected for this purpose,' Vishwas said. Whenever any devotee asked Gurmeet when the granth would finally be published, he would make an excuse that he wasn't getting enough time to write it, but that it would be out very soon.

Bizarrely, Gurmeet Ram Rahim would auction vegetables grown on Dera land in Sirsa, calling it 'divine prasad'. 'Devotees would compete with each other to bid for vegetables at the auction. For one sack, people would pay as much as Rs 10 to 12 lakh. They just wanted proximity to the Dera chief. I too once purchased a sack for Rs 2.3 lakh,' Vishwas's father said, smiling at his own foolishness. And it was the only time I saw a smile on his face during the entire length of our conversation.

The new Dera chief passed an order that every devotee had to donate 15 per cent of their income to the Dera every year. Along with this, he asked every Dera follower to keep a piggy bank at their home, and every day, put some money in it and deposit it at the Dera whenever they came for a visit.

With the Dera's continuing expansion, Gupta said Gurmeet divided the villages in Punjab, Haryana and Rajasthan where he had a considerable number of devotees into 100 blocks, with each block comprising thirty villages. Every year, three major celebrations of the cult were organized in the name of the three Dera chiefs, including Gurmeet's birthday. Each block would deposit Rs 5 lakh for each celebration per year with the headquarters.

'He completely commercialized the sect. The number of Dera followers started growing. People with vested interests, who wanted to multiply their ill-earned money, started joining the Dera, and this was when he thought of establishing factories and other commercial ventures within the Dera.'

Gupta, who by that time was considered almost family to the chief, was asked repeatedly by the latter to shift to Sirsa. In January 1997, Gupta, along with his family, shifted to Shah Satnam Ji Nagar near the Dera. This was around the time when Gurmeet started building a commercial complex in front of the old Dera. 'We were asked to invest in it and to do so, I sold my house in Karnal. He allotted a shop—Sach Shoe Centre—in my son's name. However, its profit was deposited directly with the Dera. The same was the case with other investors as well,' Gupta said.

In 1998, Gurmeet announced the opening of several factories on the Dera land. These included factories to manufacture biscuits, tomato sauce and candy. The products were sold under the brand name 'Father'. Perhaps the English translation of 'Pitaji'—which is what people called Gurmeet Ram Rahim—it was an attempt to make it appear classy. Gurmeet made Vishwas the proprietor of the biscuit factory. A given, perhaps, because his father had sold fifteen acres of ancestral agricultural land in Gharaunda to fund the factory.

Gupta said most of these factories were either nonstarters or their products were sold to Dera followers at fixed rates. On and off, some of the profits would trickle down to the actual investors, perhaps to gain their confidence. Investors who were of a higher economic status were given more of the share so that they could be primed for future investment too.

Vishwas was now a primary member of Gurmeet's entourage. At this point in our conversation, he shared with us how the Dera chief devised new methods to fleece his devotees. Gurmeet had a theatre constructed in the Dera premises where sermons and reels related to the Dera were played. Days would be chosen when it was announced that the chief would himself be coming to watch the shows. Tickets would be auctioned and people who paid the highest amount would win the 'privilege' of sitting next to the Dera chief himself.

'The highest tickets were priced at Rs 5 lakh,' he said. When I asked him why on earth people would be willing to part with that kind of money, he said, 'Look at what we were. There was a time when we were ready to die for him. What is money when such madness takes over?'

Gurmeet would organize '*rubaroo*' (face-to-face) shows in his areas of influence. The pricing of tickets was done in the same way. 'Those sitting in the first row had to pay a premium. Most of the time, his mind seemed to be making plans on how to fleece his followers,' Vishwas said. His father narrated one incident when Gurmeet came to his house for lunch and inquired about his remaining property. Gupta told him that he owned some three acres of land in the main market in Gharaunda city. The chief asked him to immediately sell that land at whatever price and invest in Dera ventures.

'When I said that I had kept it for my retirement, he told me I will get manifold returns as he had seen a vision of the Sant himself.' Gupta sold that land and handed over the money to the Dera.

Through our conversation thus far, I noticed that whenever I posed a question about Honeypreet, both father and son appeared embarrassed and skirted the topic. After a few hours, I finally managed to get them to open up about the marriage that had completely shattered the family.

'On 12 February 1999, Gurmeet called me and announced that he had fixed Vishwas's marriage with a girl of his choice, called Priyanka Taneja. The date of the marriage was two days later, on 14 February,' Gupta said. The family had never met the prospective bride, but since they never questioned Gurmeet, they agreed to this too. All the information they could gather in this period was that Priyanka's family were also ardent devotees of the Dera, and her father, Ramanand, had invested in one of the factories run by the sect.

On 14 February 1999, both the families reached the Sirsa Dera. Vishwas's father said that just before the wedding ritual was to be performed, Gurmeet called him inside the gufa and conveyed to him that he had changed the name of his would-be daughter-in-law to 'Honeypreet'. Gupta registered no objection.

From 1999 to 2009, Honeypreet stayed with Vishwas at his residence in Sirsa. She would accompany him whenever he travelled with Gurmeet outside Sirsa.

Now comes the contradiction. In his application for divorce and in interviews to the media, Vishwas had alleged that he had an inkling of some sort of an affair between Gurmeet and Honeypreet. He had, on several platforms, made allegations that he had seen his wife in a compromising position with the Dera chief, which was the main reason for seeking a divorce from her. But in my conversation with them, the father–son duo presented a different narrative. Gupta said that on 30 December 2009, Gurmeet came to their house in Sirsa and said that he had adopted Honeypreet as his daughter and would take her to the Dera with the permission of the family.

After a few days, when Honeypreet did not return, the family approached the Dera, only to be rebuffed. As Gupta was a well-known figure among the Dera followers, people attending the sangat began to discuss this incident. Also, the family was pressuring the Dera chief to send Honeypreet back to Vishwas.

In July 2011, through his emissaries, Gurmeet communicated an order that Vishwas should sign papers of a mutually acceptable divorce. Gupta said that he conveyed to the emissaries that all the money he had invested in the sect's ventures be returned before his son signed the papers, to which the Dera chief obviously refused.

According to Gupta, this incident was bringing disrepute to the Dera chief, so he hatched a plan to get Vishwas eliminated. In July 2011, they allegedly learnt from their sources of one such plan to eliminate the entire family and make it look like a case of suicide. Gupta sought the help of his friends from his days in government service and rented a place in Panchkula, to which they shifted on 16 July.

However, within a few days of moving to Panchkula, Vishwas realized that he was being followed by the Dera men, some of whom he knew by name and face. The family reported this at the city's Sector 14 police station, and within a month, ten Dera followers were arrested for stalking Vishwas.

Vishwas had stated, 'It was impossible for us to go out of the house. We could see Dera followers sitting in the park outside our house. They would chase our vehicle if we went out in it.'

From a Dera follower arrested for stalking Vishwas, a diary was recovered with names of various followers who had been deputed to keep a constant watch on Vishwas's movements. It also contained the details of places that Vishwas had visited after moving to Panchkula. Considering the seriousness of the situation, the police provided a gunman for Vishwas's security.

Concerned by the continuous threat to his life, Vishwas filed a writ petition in the Punjab and Haryana High Court, Chandigarh, on 3 October 2011, citing the incidents of stalking and harassment. The very day, he held a press conference in Chandigarh and narrated before the media the ordeal his family was undergoing, and also the criminal activities of the Dera chief.

Gurmeet was rattled. Exactly how much became apparent on 12 December 2011, when a case of dowry harassment was filed by Honeypreet in Sirsa against Vishwas, his father and his mother.

'We were scared. We went into hiding. For three months, we were in Dehradun while trying to get anticipatory bail, which was finally granted to us,' said Gupta. The horror of those days was still perceptible on Vishwas's face. A second case, this time of domestic violence, was filed against the family in Sirsa on 15 March 2012.

Even as the family was embroiled in the two cases of dowry and domestic violence for fourteen months, another FIR (first information report) under Section 420/406 was filed against Vishwas for forgery and fraud. This time, the FIR was filed by a Dera devotee in Sohana police station of Mohali. He accused Vishwas of taking a loan of Rs 25 lakh from him and giving him a cheque that had bounced.

'When we left Sirsa, I had left all my chequebooks at the factory. As I was travelling with Gurmeet most of the time, for ease of business, many of these cheques were signed for business purposes and left at the factory. One such cheque was used in this case to frame me.'

Vishwas was arrested and sent to Patiala jail, where he was lodged for fifteen days. His father got a call from a friend at the Dera who told him that a plan had been hatched to eliminate Vishwas in jail so that no one could point a finger at the Dera chief for his murder.

'I panicked and rushed to the jail. I told the entire story to the superintendent there, who, coincidentally, was from Karnal,' Gupta said. The superintendent shifted Vishwas from the common ward to a special cell where high-profile convicts were lodged.

Vishwas was lodged in the same cell as Balwant Singh Rajoana, a co-accused in the murder of Beant Singh, the twelfth chief minister of Punjab. On 28 March, a Chandigarh court sentenced Balwant Singh to death. The

Government of India stayed the execution after Punjab Chief Minister Parkash Singh Badal met President Pratibha Patil, seeking clemency. Rajoana remains on death row, with a mercy petition filed on his behalf by the SGPC (Shiromani Gurdwara Parbandhak Committee) pending with the President of India.

Rajoana was something of a hero in the jail—feared and revered in equal measure by fellow inmates. It was Rajoana who learnt about a contract given to a jail inmate to eliminate Vishwas. He took Vishwas into confidence, and, along with him, approached the jail authorities. The matter was leaked to the local media and carried in the local papers. Thus, the plot to assassinate Vishwas within the jail was foiled.

The Gupta family was fighting three legal battles simultaneously when a fourth one was added to the mix. This time, the FIR was filed against Vishwas in Hanumangarh district of Rajasthan, also by a Dera follower. The nature of the complaint was similar to the case filed in Mohali. Vishwas was accused by the complainant of duping him of Rs 10 lakh and the cheque used as evidence was from the same chequebook which, according to Vishwas, he had left at the factory in the Dera.

'We were completely shattered, financially and physically. Travelling to three different places and fighting these cases had drained us,' said Gupta.

The strain on their financial resources was immense. They had to ask relatives to help them out. Things seemed to be coming to a pass where they felt they might have no options left other than to languish in jail or commit suicide.

Seeing no respite, Vishwas's father contacted the Dera chief in September 2014. He told Gurmeet that he was willing to do anything, but wanted the safety of his family guaranteed and all the cases against them withdrawn. The Dera chief put forth two conditions— one, that Gupta and his son Vishwas apologize in front of the Dera followers during a sangat, and two, that he register his property at the Dera, which was located in a posh part of the Dera premises known as the Satguru complex.

Gupta agreed to both the conditions. Though it meant utter humiliation for him, all he could think about at that time was the safety and well-being of his only son and his family.

Gupta took his son along with him to the Dera, where a lawyer handed him a detailed note and asked him to recite it in front of the congregation. 'We wept with humiliation, but had no choice. We did as we were told.' On 16 September 2014, he transferred the said property in the name of Dera Sacha Sauda.

'He wanted us to beg on the road and he ensured that we had nothing left.' Gupta could barely keep his tears in check as he recounted this last bit.

The next day, after the registry of the property, the mutual divorce case was finalized between Vishwas and Honeypreet. The following day, the cases of dowry and domestic violence against the Gupta family were withdrawn. In a similar fashion, all the cases against the Gupta family were withdrawn within a span of one year.

The family had, since then, lived in anonymity. It was only in 2017, with the spotlight on Honeypreet, that the family came under media scrutiny. 'We had to come out with our side of the story. We wanted to tell the world the circumstances under which we had to apologize to the Dera chief,' Vishwas said. The father–son duo also dismisses many of the theories doing the rounds about Honeypreet. 'The allegation that she had women sent to Gurmeet are totally baseless as far as I know,' Vishwas said.

The family also had nothing to say against Gurmeet's family members. His biological children—two daughters and a son—were just enjoying the ill-gotten money of their father, but had nothing to do with his illegal deals.

When I asked Vishwas how he saw his future, he replied dejectedly, 'I have no hope left. The media coverage of Honeypreet and the salacious reports have only served to worsen my life.' Having spent much of his youth with Gurmeet, his studies had suffered and he was unable to get a job. Since all their money had been taken away by the Dera chief, Vishwas couldn't even open a small shop to support his family. He said he sometimes felt like ending his life, but the thought of his three-month-old daughter stopped him from taking that extreme step.

The family lives on the small pension that Gupta receives. It has cut almost all its ties with relatives and friends because wherever they go, the topic of conversation invariably turns to Honeypreet.

'We have nothing to say against her now. The law will take its own course,' said Vishwas.

Gupta, who invested a major part of his life and money in the Dera, still hasn't lost his faith in Shah Satnam. 'Even if the whole world stands on one side, I will stand by the side of my Guruji Shah Satnam. I still see him when I meditate,' he said. His greatest regret is not leaving the Dera when 'this monster took over'.

Part III

The Long Road to Justice

Part III

The Long Road to Justice

A Journalist Is Silenced

For twenty-one-year-old Anshul, life was moving at a pace that any youngster from a small town envisions. He was good at his studies and dreamt of studying to be a lawyer. It was his father's dream that he was pursuing diligently. With two siblings—a fourteen-year-old brother, Aridman, and sixteen-year-old sister, Shreyasi—mother Kulwant Kaur and father Ram Chander Chhatrapati, Anshul was content and secure. Little did he know that life as he knew it and expected it to be was about to change forever.

After 8.15 p.m. on 24 October 2002, he would embark on the journey of a relentless legal battle, fought amid constant threats to him and his family. He was not to know that for the next fifteen years, he would have to put aside his own dreams and fight tooth and nail for justice for his family.

On that fateful day, in their small, single-storeyed house at Govind Nagar in Sirsa, Anshul was watching a television show along with his brother and sister. He was also chopping vegetables for the dinner that was yet to be made. His mother had had to leave in a hurry that morning for Guru Har Sahai in Firozpur, Punjab, to attend the funeral of a close family member. Before leaving, she had instructed Anshul to take care of his younger siblings for she was aware of her husband's routine of returning home late from work.

'After writing his reports and sending the newspaper to press, my father had a habit of meeting his old friends at a tea shop in town. There, he would discuss the latest news making the rounds, and also take feedback on major events taking place at the Dera.'

That day, however, was not a usual one. Chhatrapati, to his children's surprise, reached home at around 7.15 p.m., which was early for him. He was elated as he told Anshul about a major lead in his investigation against Gurmeet Ram Rahim Singh. He announced that he would try his culinary skills and busied himself in the kitchen.

At around 8.05 p.m., the family heard a motorcycle stop at their gate and someone call for Ram Chander Chhatrapati by name from the small alley outside their house. Asking his children to stay indoors, he went out to meet the visitor. The house has two gates—a bigger one, which opens out into the main alley of the locality to the west, and a smaller one, which opens into an adjoining alley to the north of the house. Normally, the main gate was kept closed most of the time, and it was the smaller gate that was used by the family to enter and exit the house.

As was his habit, this time too, Chhatrapati used the smaller gate to get out of the house. The killers, who had obviously been tracking his and his family's movements, knew that it was the small gate that was in frequent use. If they waited for him at that gate, Chhatrapati might not open it. So they hid themselves behind the main gate on the west side, and waited for him to emerge from the small gate and walk out towards the main alley.

When a few minutes had passed, Anshul thought of going out and calling his father back in for dinner. He was about to open the main door when they all heard five consecutive gunshots. The assailants, two in number, fled the spot on a motorcycle. As the nearest police post at Khairpur was barely 200 metres from the house, one of the assailants, Kuldeep Singh, was apprehended by a constable who had heard the gunshots and was heading towards the alley. The other assailant, Nirmal Singh, managed to flee the crime scene.

Meanwhile, Anshul locked the main door of the house and rushed towards the small gate.

'By the time I reached the main alley, all I could see was my father lying in a pool of blood.' He started screaming for help as he rushed to help his father. Chhatrapati, though grievously wounded, with two gunshots in the abdomen and one each on the shoulder, the back and the thigh, was trying to stand up. The entire neighbourhood had heard the gunshots and people had started gathering in the alley. A neighbour brought his car out and rushed the badly wounded Chhatrapati to the nearest hospital in Sirsa.

The doctors at the civil hospital were ill-equipped to deal with the grievous bullet injuries, and, after providing preliminary medical aid, asked for Chhatrapati to be shifted to Pandit Bhagwat Dayal Sharma Post Graduate Institute of Medical Sciences (PGIMS) at Rohtak. Anshul, along with some close friends of his father, organized the move.

'The 200–km drive from Sirsa to Rohtak seemed like the longest I have ever had to drive in my life. All throughout, I was holding my father's hand. He was conscious and was looking into my eyes. I felt utterly miserable and helpless,' said the son, for whom his father was the greatest role model.

Meanwhile, Anshul's sister and brother were at home, crying and clueless about why their father had been shot. The news of the brutal attack also reached Firozpur. Kulwant Kaur composed herself and started for Rohtak. 'He was an upright man. He was fighting against a monster and he knew its consequences,' Kaur told me while recalling that night of horror. 'He would always tell us that no one has left this earth alive. "Neither will I. But I can't sit back and see my city go to ruin because of Gurmeet Ram Rahim."'

After being shifted to PGIMS, over the next few days, Chhatrapati's condition remained critical, even though he had occasional periods of consciousness. However, on 7 November, he slipped into a semi-coma and stopped responding to treatment.

During this period at PGIMS, Anshul got first-hand experience of the Sirsa Police being under the influence of the Dera chief. He also realized that it would be a long fight for him to get the people responsible for the attack on his father punished. On 26 October, a subinspector (SI) from the Sirsa Police, Ram Chander, had visited PGIMS to record Chhatrapati's statement after Anshul told the local administration in Sirsa that his father was conscious and could identify his attackers.

Anshul was in the emergency room where the subinspector was recording his father's statement. 'My father categorically told him that Gurmeet Ram Rahim was the mastermind of this attack. It was his henchman who shot at him.'

However, when Anshul checked the papers on which the SI was supposed to have recorded the statement, he noticed that the name of Gurmeet Ram Rahim Singh was mentioned nowhere. He confronted the SI in front of his father right there in the emergency room, to which the latter said that he would make a detailed report sitting outside the room. He promised Anshul that the Dera chief's name would be included.

Anshul later found out that in the FIR filed in this case with the Sirsa Police, the Dera chief's name was omitted. Anshul's claim is corroborated by a portion of the charge sheet filed by the CBI in the Chhatrapati murder case. This states, 'The same subinspector was subjected to polygraph test at CFSL (Central Forensic Science Laboratory), New Delhi, in 2005. The test revealed deception in his statement. Subsequently, he was again subjected to the test on the intervening night of May 16/17, 2007, and deception was again noticed in his statement. This clearly makes out Anshul Chhatrapati is telling the truth.'

With Chhatrapati's condition worsening and no immediate prospects of improvement, Anshul was advised to shift his father once again, this time to Apollo Hospital in Delhi. On 8 November, when he was being taken to Delhi, Chhatrapati asked Anshul, 'Where are you taking me?' These were his last words. He was put on life support at Apollo, where, on 21 November, the brave journalist breathed his last.

The news of Chhatrapati's death reached Sirsa and, within minutes, had spread through the town like wildfire. The otherwise quiet town was simmering with rage. Within no time, people gathered on the streets. They included members of the local bar association, traders and other common people. This was a defining moment in the quest to bring Gurmeet Ram Rahim Singh to justice. For the first time since the establishment of Dera Sacha Sauda in Sirsa, people were out on the streets chanting anti-Dera slogans. It was also the first time the Dera's authority had been challenged on such a large scale in Sirsa.

Chhatrapati was born on 19 March 1950 in Raniwala in Firozpur district of Punjab. Later, his parents shifted to Darbi village in Sirsa district. He went for higher education to Indore University and got a degree in law. During his college days, he was known for his poetry, most of which was about the class struggle and the government's failure to ensure a life of dignity and equality for its citizens. One such poem, '*Mujhko Sarkar Banane Do*' (Let Me Form the Government), was quite a hit among his peers. In this poem, he takes a dig at the government and administration for failing the marginalized in society. He was the editor of the college magazine *Raj Dharam* for two consecutive years and was known for his stinging editorials aimed at the ruling dispensation.

After returning to Sirsa, Chhatrapati began practising law at the local court and was known as a fierce champion of human rights. 'He was made of something different. A blend of an idealist and a socialist,' Gurjeet Singh, a lawyer who shifted base from Sirsa to Delhi in 2003, told me.

People who were close to Chhatrapati vouch for the fact that his first love was journalism. He would write on social issues even while practising law, and was eventually appointed district correspondent of *Samar Ghosh* in 1996. Noticing his distinct style of writing and his hold on local issues, the newspaper allocated him a column named 'Pratidin' (Daily). 'Pratidin' became an instant hit because of Chhatrapati's guts and gumption in taking the local administration and politicians head-on.

'There was a time when we used to subscribe to *Samar Ghosh* only to read Chhatrapati's write-ups,' remembered seventy-two-year-old Gurpal Singh, who runs a small grocery near Sirsa's bus stand.

In 1998, a child was run over by a jeep in Begu village, adjoining Sirsa. Investigation by the local press revealed that the jeep was owned by Dera Sacha Sauda. Chhatrapati took the lead on this and got it prominently published in the local dailies. This was the first time he realized the might of the Dera. The local newspaper representatives, including Chhatrapati, were threatened by the Dera supporters. However, due to mounting pressure from residents, a meeting of journalists and the management committee of the Dera was organized and a compromise reached after the latter agreed to provide a written apology. Chhatrapati had been at the forefront in this matter and represented the local journalists. He therefore became an eyesore for the Dera chief.

Meanwhile, after stints at various state- and district-level newspapers, Chhatrapati started working on his long-held desire to start his own newspaper. He discussed it with his family and after arranging the minimum amount required, from sources like his farm income and his wife's savings, he gathered together a motley group of rookie journalists and announced the commencement of a four-page eveninger, *Poora Sach*. One reason for naming the eveninger *Poora Sach*, apart from the obvious centrality of truth to journalism, was to counter a daily called *Sach*, which was then published by the Dera followers in Sirsa.

From 2 February 2000 onwards, *Poora Sach* became operational from a ramshackle building situated in Court Colony, Sirsa. His close friends said that after a long session of brainstorming with them, Chhatrapati said that his eveninger should always be known for bringing all the facts into the public domain. The name *Poora Sach* was thought to be apt and was finalized.

Within one month of its launch, *Poora Sach* was already giving stiff competition to other dailies. The reason for its growing popularity was its tone, which was non-partisan, and its content, which was hard-hitting. People close to Chhatrapati reveal that he was always concerned about the growing clout of the Dera. Chhatrapati started investigating how, despite the Dera not accepting any alms from followers, its economic power was growing from strength to strength. He also grew suspicious about the fact that people owning land near the Dera were either selling their land to the Dera at throwaway prices or were simply gifting their land to the sect. He smelled foul play. He also wondered about people working for more than fifteen hours without getting paid anything for their labour. These things baffled him. He used to tell his friends that it could not be just a matter of faith, and that something bigger and more sinister was brewing at Dera Sacha Sauda.

From time to time, *Poora Sach* carried articles related to illegal land-grabbing and other news coming out of the Dera. Chhatrapati also published reports about how the Dera followers were engaged in power theft, especially those followers living on the roads leading to the Dera. His news reports were backed by concrete evidence, and the Dera, on most occasions, failed to counter his reports convincingly.

Chhatrapati had his sources at the Dera, who were willing to spill the beans about Gurmeet Ram Rahim but were not willing to come on record. He was also working on leads related to the unsolved murders and mysterious deaths of Dera followers. A Sirsa bar council member, a close friend of Chhatrapati, told me that Chhatrapati always had a hunch that the Dera was becoming a den of nefarious activities under Gurmeet Ram Rahim. He even went inside the Dera in disguise several times during the course of his investigation. He was collecting evidence against the Dera chief and was sitting on a big scoop.

Even as Chhatrapati was relentlessly pursuing stories related to the Dera and publishing them in *Poora Sach*, on 30 May 2002, during the early hours of the day at Rodi market in Sirsa, a car driver clashed with a local cop. During a search of the car, the cop recovered photostat copies of the anonymous letter written by the sadhvi, accusing the Dera chief of sexual exploitation.

'The letter was already in circulation in Sirsa. It had been posted to the offices of some local dailies, including one located in the Kurukshetra district of Haryana,' says Lekhraj Doth, a long-term associate of Chhatrapati from his days of practising law. 'Chhatrapati got to know about this and managed to get a hold of a copy of the letter.'

The same day, *Poora Sach* published the letter verbatim. It also carried a supporting report titled '*Dharam Ke Naam Pe Kiye Jaa Rahe Hain Sadhviyon Ke Jeevan Barbaad*' (In the Name of Religion, the Lives of Sadhvis Are Being Destroyed). The accompanying report incorporated details from Chhatrapati's investigation. Another newspaper, *Lekha Jokha* (The Chronicle), an evening newspaper published from Fatehabad, also published the details of the letter.

The moment these newspapers hit the stands in the evening, the letter became a hot topic of discussion in Sirsa and adjoining areas. Though many people would speculate about illegal activities at the Dera, this was the first time that Gurmeet Ram Rahim had been named and exposed in such a direct and detailed manner.

'Within minutes of *Poora Sach* hitting the stands, copies of the newspaper were picked up by the Dera followers and burnt at the crossroads in Sirsa,' Amrut Singh, who made his living as a newspaper vendor in those days, recalled. 'We reached the office of *Poora Sach* and demanded more copies.'

The office of *Lekha Jokha* in Fatehabad was attacked the same day and employees badly injured by the Dera disciples. The attackers were armed with sticks, rods and canisters of petrol. Their intention was to burn the newspaper's office. However, the tragedy was averted by the timely intervention of the local police. Meanwhile, in Sirsa, Chhatrapati and his friends guarded the office of *Poora Sach* the whole evening and the next day so as to avert any such incident. This much was clear—Chhatrapati was now in direct confrontation with the Dera chief.

Apprehending a threat to his life from the Dera's henchmen, Chhatrapati wrote a letter to the superintendent of police, Sirsa, on 2 July 2002. The letter clearly outlined the fact that he was facing a threat to his life because of the series of exposés against the Dera chief. In the letter, Chhatrapati mentioned how, after publishing the anonymous letter, he was getting threatening calls, some of them blatant ones and others somewhat subtle. He was apprehensive that his daily routine was being tracked by Gurmeet Ram Rahim's henchmen. With a wife and three children at home, and without any proper security, his family could also be made a target in order to silence his pen.

The letter kept lying in the SP's office and its seriousness was ignored.

It was only when he was rummaging through his father's papers that Anshul recovered a copy of that letter. He said that his father never wanted his family to be worried round-the-clock about his safety, which was why he never told them about that letter or the numerous threats to his life. Friends who dropped in at their house did make a point about taking greater security precautions.

It was during this time that the Dera chief's troubleshooters approached Chhatrapati through common acquaintances. Just fifteen days before he was shot, Krishan Lal, the Dera's manager, contacted Chhatrapati to convince him to cut a deal with Gurmeet Ram Rahim.

Anshul recalls a conversation that his father had with one of his friends while he was facing threats to his life from the Dera followers. When his friend expressed concern at the threats, Chhatrapati responded, 'The kind of journalism I am doing, I am sure people will not merely beat me up. I am going to be shot dead.'

Recalling a meeting with Chhatrapati, Yogendra Yadav, an eminent academic and psephologist, told me, 'Whenever I listen about any news related to Dera Sacha Sauda, I recall the date of 20 October 2002. That day, I was in Sirsa. I was invited to take part in a seminar on

"Alternative Politics and the Role of the Media", organized by the editor of *Poora Sach*, Ram Chander Chhatrapati. I was impressed by the honesty and bravery for which Chhatrapati was famous in Sirsa. His popularity in Hindi and Punjabi literary circles in the area was one more thing that impressed me.

'After delivering my lecture, he took me out for a treat of dahi-jalebi. There, sitting at the roadside, he told me about the illegal activities taking place inside the Dera. He told me about the sexual exploitation of a sadhvi inside the Dera. I asked Chhatrapati if this was religion, then what is iniquity? To which he laughed and said that no one has enough courage to speak the truth. Some are keeping quiet as speaking against the Dera chief might hit their vote bank, and some are silent because of the greed for money. However, in *Poora Sach*, Chhatrapati said that he had published the anonymous letter written by the sadhvi. He said that within a month of the anonymous letter being in the public domain, the brother of a sadhvi, Ranjit Singh, was murdered. I asked him, "Ram Chander, is there a threat to your life as well?" To which he replied, "Yes, I have received several life threats. Don't know what will happen. But one day, everyone has to go." After four days, I heard the news that Chhatrapati had been shot at five times in front of his house.'

It was during this seminar, which Yogendra Yadav referred to, that Chhatrapati said he was clueless why his fellow journalists were not able to write fearlessly (about the Dera). He said that they had the capability and the power of the pen, and he was sure that the day would come when his fellow journalists would write fearlessly and emphatically.

A day before Chhatrapati was shot, Gurmeet Ram Rahim had come back to the Dera from Jalandhar. The Dera chief was shown the many editions of *Poora Sach*, including the one in which the anonymous letter by the sadhvi was published. Articles against the Dera were monitored by Krishan Lal, a right-hand aide of Gurmeet, who was also appointed manager of the day-to-day affairs of the Dera. On 23 October too, Chhatrapati had published an article against the Dera chief.

It was evening and Gurmeet was sitting with his confidants in his infamous gufa when Krishan showed him clippings of articles published against him by Chhatrapati. It was then that a criminal conspiracy was hatched to eliminate Chhatrapati. Carpenters by profession and part of the Dera chief's inner circle, Kuldeep Singh and Nirmal Singh were summoned to the gufa. Both the assailants had previously been trained at the Dera to handle small arms and target shooting.

The would-be assailants were given small weapons, which included a licensed revolver of Krishan Lal's. On the day of the assault, they were also given a walkie-talkie set, issued in the name of the Dera, to inform Krishan Lal once the task was complete.

A CBI officer who was part of the team investigating the murder of Chhatrapati said, 'Chhatrapati had been on

Gurmeet's radar for a long time. Gurmeet finally decided that Chhatrapati should be eliminated on 23 October.'

And the assassination was carried out as per the plan.

While Anshul was busy with his father's funeral in Sirsa, the local police seemed to be working overtime to save the Dera chief from any controversy. The FIR in this murder case had no mention of the Dera chief. This, even after the fact that the second assailant, Nirmal Singh, was also nabbed the day after the murder. From him, the police had recovered the licensed weapon issued in the name of the Dera manager Krishan Lal, and a walkie-talkie issued in the name of Dera Sacha Sauda.

The theory peddled by the local police was that Chhatrapati was murdered because of a family feud. Lekhraj, who, along with his colleague, was constantly monitoring the police investigation, was in shock when he learnt that despite all the evidence pointing at the involvement of the Dera chief in the murder, his name was mentioned nowhere in the FIR.

'The police was trying to divert [attention from] the issue. According to them, it was a relative of Kulwant Kaur who had hired these assassins for the murder over a land dispute in Kulwant's paternal village,' Lekhraj said.

Anshul, who was yet to recover from the shock of his father's murder, had two new challenges before him. First, to keep *Poora Sach* functioning, and second, to ensure that the investigation into the murder proceeded in the correct direction. He started monitoring the editorial work of the newspaper. 'I had no option but to leave my studies. The family was grieving, there was a constant threat to our lives, and I had to take care of my brother and sister. I had to focus on what was at hand.'

Anshul made numerous visits to state authorities and local politicians to ensure a free and fair investigation, but it seemed in vain. 'It used to break my faith at times when I used to see local politicians heading towards the Dera to seek this monster's blessings, while we were left to fight on our own.'

The Dera chief, meanwhile, was not letting go of any opportunity to malign Chhatrapati. Within a month of his murder, a '*peela parcha*' (yellow pamphlet) mysteriously appeared in circulation in Sirsa. Thousands of Dera supporters started distributing these pamphlets in the main markets of Sirsa. The first thing people noticed at their doorstep in the morning was this pamphlet. The pamphlet contained obscene language and allegations of blackmail and extramarital affairs against Chhatrapati. It was alleged that the journalist had been murdered because of the reasons mentioned in the pamphlet.

Later, during the course of the investigation, it was found that a Dera supporter, Praveen Singh, was behind this mischief. He was instructed by the Dera chief to dent Chhatrapati's impeccable reputation so that the investigation into his murder could be diverted.

'The content of the pamphlet was so vile that it can't even be discussed. As Chhatrapati and his work were well-known in the city, no one took it seriously,' Lekhraj Doth told me.

The Dera also used its might to put a clamp on the publication of *Poora Sach*, which, at that point, was going at full throttle to unmask the Dera. With Anshul at the helm of affairs, no news related to the Dera was spared. The sponsors of *Poora Sach* were threatened, as a result of which, many of them dissociated themselves from the eveninger. Its vendors were beaten up and copies were seized and burnt.

Anshul was hard-pressed for funds to keep the paper going. A major part of the earnings from the small farmland the family had went into meeting the expenses of the paper. 'There was no revenue. *Poora Sach* continued writing against the establishment and the Dera. We made it a point to update our readers on the progress of the case and I regularly wrote editorials,' said Anshul.

With the local administration in cahoots with the Dera, Anshul's almost single-handed fight against Gurmeet Ram Rahim was proving to be a Herculean task. This was when Anshul, along with a few of his father's friends, started a signature campaign in Sirsa to hand the case over to the CBI. The signature campaign proved to be an extraordinary idea and many NGOs also joined in.

In January 2003, Anshul petitioned the Punjab and Haryana High Court for a CBI investigation into the case. After nine months of waiting, the court finally accepted the petition and the investigation was handed over to the CBI.

A conclusive presentation of evidence was made by the CBI in November 2014 in court, along with evidence in the murder case of Ranjit Singh.

While the CBI investigation was on, Anshul and his family were still under constant peril. During the course of the *Tehelka* investigation, when we met Anshul for the first time, the first thing we noticed about him was his tenacity. We agreed to meet at his lawyer's house since he had recently received a threat from the Dera and did not want to expose us to the Dera's henchmen, who were tracking his movements.

During the course of our meeting, he showed us the newspapers cuttings and articles written by his father and him against the Dera chief. When we revealed the actual purpose of our visit, he was more than happy to assist us. I vividly remember him saying, *'Sir, poori jaan laga denge. Iss criminal ko bachhna nahin chahiye.'* (We'll try very hard. This criminal should not go unpunished.)

After meeting Anshul, we realized how tough it must have been for him to challenge a fake godman who literally owned half the city. 'I don't have anywhere near the muscle power that Gurmeet has. There are days when I have to shut my family indoors for days due to reports that I get of a possible attack on us,' he told us during the several meetings that we had in 2007. The academic performance of his siblings was also affected due to the constant stress and harassment they faced from the Dera followers.

If the killing of his father was not enough, Anshul and his family were subjected to another form of torture when

Gurmeet started appearing on news channels and silver screens after 2013. 'We used to sit helplessly and watch the murderer of my father being eulogized by prominent anchors on national TV channels,' he said. The family was distraught at the fact that a person who was accused of rape and murder was being endowed with the halo of a saviour and a god.

'I used to get enraged at those images. He was throwing money to buy the media and here we were, just somehow managing to run *Poora Sach* with our meagre finances to fight him.'

Ultimately, the lack of funds and support from advertisers forced the family to shut down *Poora Sach*. Anshul started concentrating on the family farm as they needed money for his siblings' higher studies. During this entire period, through many intermediaries, the family was offered money by the Dera to withdraw the murder case.

'My family's only purpose of living was to see the murderers of my father behind bars. And this intention was clearly conveyed to the intermediaries,' Anshul told me during a conversation in late 2015.

For fifteen long years, the family abstained from any kind of celebration. However, on 28 August 2017, when the Dera chief was sentenced to twenty years in prison in the rape cases, Anshul distributed sweets in his locality. Interviews with him were aired on most national news channels. And everywhere, he was heard saying, 'This is just the beginning. Now I am waiting for the Dera chief to be convicted of my father's murder.'

I called Anshul to congratulate him on this first victory. The joy in his voice was obvious. Besides other conversation related to the case, I asked him about *Poora Sach*. 'Sir, now, first I will enrol in a law course. And second, I will revive the newspaper.'

I remembered then his words, which I had often heard him repeat over the years: *'Sach aur jhooth ke beech koi teesri cheez nahin hoti, mere pitaji yahi kehte the.'* (There is no third thing between truth and falsehood, that is what my father used to say.)

The Investigator

'Three young members of Parliament [MPs] from the Congress party were after me to close the cases against Gurmeet Ram Rahim Singh.' A former CBI top cop now in his late sixties, Mulinja Narayanan, made this startling revelation while talking to me. 'Two MPs were from Haryana and one from Rajasthan.' He disclosed the names of these three young MPs, but asked me to keep it off the record. 'I don't want to invite any controversy now. This might become an issue of one political party against another. The point here is that Gurmeet Ram Rahim was shielded over the years by political parties, be it Congress or the ruling BJP.'

Narayanan was the deputy inspector general (DIG), Special Crimes Region, in late 2006 when he was handed the investigation into the rape and murder charges against Gurmeet Singh. Narayanan was hand-picked by the then CBI chief Vijay Shanker. The CBI was reprimanded by the Punjab and

Haryana High Court for the slow pace of its investigation into the cases, and Shanker wanted an officer with an impeccable record to handle the case. Within the agency, Narayanan was known as a tough cookie who didn't buckle under pressure. When he was handed the case, Narayanan knew that it would involve braving a lot of pressure from politicians, especially those from Punjab and Haryana—states where the Dera had the largest number of followers.

'During those days, we had inputs that Gurmeet had influence on twenty-four assembly seats and he was on the hotline with some of the top politicians of the country. I knew that by 2014, he was in a position to swing the fate of political parties with his influence on twenty-eight seats, comprising seats in Punjab, Haryana and Rajasthan.' Apart from political pressure, he knew that the Sirsa Police and some top cops were 'eating out of the hands' of Gurmeet Singh. The investigation into the various cases, which began in 2002, was marred by deliberately shoddy slip-ups. But these were not the only hurdles Narayanan was going to face. The immediate challenge for him was to get on record the statements of the sadhvis who alleged rape by the Dera chief.

'Most of the sadhvis who had left the Dera were married and many had children. Getting them to speak to us was the biggest issue the agency was facing. Those who wanted to come on record were silenced by their own family members.'

If this was not enough, some of Narayanan's superior officers were also keen that he close the cases against the

Dera chief. Narayanan said that the day he was handed the cases, two senior officers barged into his room and asked him to close the cases without a probe.

'The day I was assigned the case, two of my superiors walked into my room and said that this case was being given to me for closing.' He told his superiors that he did not take instructions from them and the case had been handed to him after the court ordered that it be given to someone at the CBI who would not be unduly influenced.

'I told them that the investigation will go on as per the law. The FIR had been registered in 2002, but for years, nothing had moved. I then told them that they could leave my room.' Narayanan recalled that one of the two senior officers humiliated him for a while, and then left the room fuming. Later, they also tried to pressure his team members, but in vain.

One of the first things he received was an application, in which one of the sadhvis who had given a statement against the Dera chief in the case of the murder of Ranjit Singh had requested for adequate security for her and her family. This request was made by the sadhvi after the agency had successfully traced two of the sadhvis who had been subjected to sexual exploitation by Gurmeet Ram Rahim. Though the sadhvi who asked for security was yet to record her statement in the rape case, she feared for her life and she expressed the same fear to the CBI sleuths who were handling the case before Narayanan.

'I was amazed at why she wasn't given security. It could have helped us gain her confidence. She was to be given the assurance,' he said. Narayanan said he summoned the officer concerned and reprimanded him for this laxity. The sadhvi was immediately given protection.

Narayanan then contacted the father of this sadhvi and fixed a meeting. The father feared a backlash from the Dera disciples, but a major concern was one of honour—how would he face the world once it was out in the open that his daughter had been raped? 'I told him that by keeping quiet, they were endangering the lives of hundreds of sadhvis who were still residing in the Dera premises.'

Narayanan told the father that he should ask his daughter to record her statement with the CBI for the greater good of society. As her husband was not aware of the rape, her father was worried what would happen once her husband came to know the truth. Narayanan said that when he spoke to the sadhvi, 'she showed signs of coming on record, but was scared because of obvious reasons'. He said that he played the role of a father figure for her and assured her that come what may, no harm would come to her.

Narayanan assured her father that he would personally meet the woman's husband and convince him that being raped was not her fault and that it was the rapist who should be ashamed. 'I met the husband along with the survivor's father. He threatened to divorce her if she recorded her statement. It came as a shock to him that this was kept a secret from him.'

In the meantime, Narayanan and his team met former sadhvis who had left in the last five years and could possibly be victims of sexual exploitation at the Dera. Most of them, though, said that they knew that sadhvis were sexually exploited at the Dera but they were not among them. These former sadhvis were married, and the fear that their married lives would be ruined was one of the reasons they refused to cooperate with the agency. Some of the former sadhvis who were approached by the CBI even complained to the National Commission for Women (NCW) that they were being harassed by the CBI. The CBI was, in turn, questioned by the NCW.

Narayanan met the NCW officials and filled them in on the developments in the case. 'We brought them into the loop and requested them to convince the former sadhvis to come out and speak the truth, otherwise this rapist would never be brought to book.'

Sensing the gravity of the issue, the NCW team met a few victims along with the CBI and tried to convince them, including the one who finally recorded her statement. Narayanan knew, after multiple meetings with one of the survivors, that if her husband was convinced, the woman might possibly come on record, and it finally paid off.

Though the family of this sadhvi agreed to cooperate with the CBI, their condition was that she would not reveal her identity in open court. To record her statement, the sadhvi and her family were to be taken to a CBI special court in Ambala. This was a major challenge for the agency. The Dera followers were monitoring the house of this sadhvi round the clock. The chances were high that the team would have a violent encounter with the Dera followers during the move from her house to Ambala. The Dera followers who had mounted surveillance on the sadhvi's house heavily outnumbered the CBI team. Also, thus far, the local police had failed to help the agency make much headway.

Narayanan said that it was at this point that a top cop in the Haryana Police came forward to help arrange vehicles and security for the sadhvi. Decoy vehicles were used to mislead the Dera followers, while the agency managed to transport the sadhvi to the court. Narayanan said, 'During the morning hours, the court is generally crowded, so special arrangements were made to record the statement in the late evening.' The statement was recorded on camera and in the chamber of the special magistrate, under Section 164 of the CrPC.

'I wanted to ensure that no one plays dirty and weakens the case later. Therefore, I got the statement of the girl recorded before a magistrate so that retracting it becomes nearly impossible.'

Buoyed by this success, the CBI started focusing on the other sadhvi whom the agency had evidence on as a rape survivor. 'Her house in Hisar was under complete siege. The Dera followers used to sleep outside her house and she was under virtual house arrest,' Narayanan said, recalling his first visit to her house.

Though the agency provided her with security, it was virtually impossible to sneak her out of the house under such a heavy deployment of Dera disciples. Her husband, who was physically disabled, told Narayanan that he wanted to kill Gurmeet Ram Rahim even if it meant being hanged after that. 'He was quite agitated and wanted to see Gurmeet behind bars.' The agency convinced him that once his wife's statement was recorded under Section 164 of the CrPC, it would be difficult for the Dera chief to escape the consequences under the law.

The agency also wanted this sadhvi to come on record to fortify the case for another reason. The first sadhvi's statement could be challenged since her brother had allegedly been murdered and the counsel for Gurmeet might try to dismiss the statement as a motivated one. But with another sadhvi coming on record, the case against Gurmeet would become much stronger. Narayanan knew this.

'It became a game of wits between us and the Dera followers. Whenever we tried to take the sadhvi out of the house, the Dera followers would surround our team.'

However, luck seemed to side with the agency. One day, the Dera chief visited Hisar to take part in a religious congregation. The followers, for a brief period, lifted their siege. This small window of time was all that the CBI needed. They hatched and executed their plan. 'We immediately moved the girl and her family to one of our safe houses,' Narayanan said.

When the Dera followers returned, they found the house empty and ransacked it.

The Dera's PR machinery swung into action and the next day, local dailies were filled with reports of how the sadhvi and her family had been 'abducted'. The local police were pressured to locate the sadhvi at the earliest. The Dera followers were instructed to find her before she recorded her statement.

The agency kept the sadhvi at the safe house for a while and, at an opportune time, took her to Ambala to record her statement. The same procedure was adopted in this case as well. Her statement was recorded on camera and during the late evening in the chamber of the magistrate. This was the second big breakthrough for the agency.

While all this was happening, the three MPs mentioned at the beginning of this chapter kept calling Narayanan and exerted pressure on him to close the case. The calls were made to his assistant, and each time, the request made was the same. 'The situation reached such a point that I had to ask my assistant to stop taking their calls. There were times when my assistant simply put the call on hold and kept them waiting at the other end.'

When they failed to influence Narayanan, the MPs took a different route. They met the CBI chief, Vijay Shanker. As per Narayanan, the chief clearly told them that the probe would proceed as per the law and political influence would not work.

Meanwhile, the Dera chief made a wrong move, according to Narayanan. He got embroiled in the controversy over impersonating Guru Gobind Singh. 'This really helped us. The Sikhs were up in arms against him. Haryana and Punjab were on the boil. The Dera chief came to the attention of the national media and political pressure on us eased a bit.'

Narayanan told me about a meeting that took place between the CBI chief and the then prime minister Manmohan Singh at the latter's official residence at 7, Race Course Road (now Lok Kalyan Marg). The meeting was called by Singh to inquire about the developments in the case against Gurmeet. He was concerned about the situation in Punjab and Haryana, where the Sikhs and Dera followers were at loggerheads. The prime minister also wanted to dig into the facts and check on the allegations made by some MPs from Punjab and Haryana that the agency was unnecessarily framing the Dera chief in cases of rape and murder.

During the meeting, the CBI chief showed him the statements of the sadhvis. The prime minister was appalled, said Narayanan. The CBI chief told Narayanan after the meeting that the PM had said the agency should go full throttle against the Dera chief and ignore any kind of political pressure. 'The then PM showed full resolve and backed us. He asked the agency to go by the law.'

There were two things at that time which were working in the agency's favour—one, the prime minister was backing the team, and two, as the case was handed over to the CBI by the court, even if the state governments wanted to play tricks, they did not have much opportunity to do so.

Here, I would like to add that after the court convicted the Dera chief in the rape cases, the ruling political party, the BJP, tried to take credit for it, saying that it was because of former prime minister Atal Bihari Vajpayee, who initiated the process of investigation against the Dera chief after the prime minister's office (PMO) received the sadhvi's anonymous letter in 2002. It is true that the PMO did receive the letter, as did many other authorities, but it was the Punjab and Haryana High Court that took cognizance of the letter and handed the case to the CBI in 2002.

Having received Prime Minister Manmohan Singh's backing, the next challenge before the CBI was to question the Dera chief based on the recorded statements of the sadhvis. 'In July, I got a call from my chief that Gurmeet Ram Rahim had agreed to be questioned, but he said that he wouldn't give us more than half an hour. He said that we had to move that very day to Sirsa immediately,' Narayanan recalled. He was in Chandigarh at that time, and travelling from there to Sirsa took a few hours.

His primary concern was the security of his own team. It was known that many top officers of the Sirsa Police were 'bhakts' (devotees) of the Dera chief, and Narayanan had little or no hope from them for their security in case the Dera followers got agitated and attacked the team.

'When we reached the Dera and met Gurmeet, he appeared very irritated. He complained that he had very little time and we should wind up the questioning at the earliest.'

Narayanan's first impression of Gurmeet was of a scared and fake godman. He had already briefed his team that time should not be a constraint and the Dera chief should be grilled till he answered all their questions, even if it took them the whole day.

'The Dera chief appeared to be scared during questioning . . . He did not give any direct reply. He pretended to be a baba, but my instincts told me that he was a scared person during the questioning.'

After the initial grilling, Gurmeet seemed to mellow down. He sat with folded hands in front of the CBI sleuths. 'We informed him that we had arrest orders from the court if he didn't cooperate with us. This really scared him and he toned it down.' The CBI grilled him for two and a half hours and all this while, he was standing in front of the team. He denied all the charges against him.

Once they left the Dera, Narayanan started getting calls from random numbers. He said that someone had leaked his number, and the tone of the calls ranged from mild to threatening. 'Not only me, but other colleagues who were part of this investigation also started getting these calls.' The numbers were later traced to remote areas of Punjab and Haryana, and the SIM cards used had been purchased using fake IDs.

After interrogating the Dera chief, the CBI filed a charge sheet against him in the last week of July at an Ambala court. The charge sheet referred to the sexual exploitation of the two sadhvis between 1999 and 2001. This charge sheet was filed just a few days after *Tehelka*'s 'Operation Jhootha Sauda' aired on India TV.

The veteran officer Narayanan, who rose from inspector to DIG before retiring in 2009, admits that this was one of the cases in his long career in which politicians approached him directly to close the probe or attempted to weaken the investigation. Though the sect had always claimed to be apolitical, Gurmeet Ram Rahim knew that having politicians on his side might help shield him from the law.

I remember that while we were conducting our investigation under Operation Jhootha Sauda, we were told by one of the former Dera followers how in 2004, a minister in Vajpayee's government was asked to wait outside the gufa for two hours because 'Baba' was not happy with her. In 2007, to capitalize on its growing clout, the Dera launched its own political wing, known as the Political Affairs Wing (PAW). The PAW was meant to 'advise' the Dera followers on which candidate or political party to vote for and support in the assembly and general elections.

'The PAW openly supported the Congress in 2007, and it was obvious that Congress leaders in the region dominated by his sect were eating out of his hands,' Narayanan said.

What took so long for the law to catch up with Gurmeet, even after the CBI had enough evidence to nail him in the rape cases?

Narayanan said that he retired in 2009, and the officers succeeding him suffered the same problems as he did. Gurmeet's clout—in terms of money, the sheer number of followers and his political patronage—just kept growing. He said that he often got calls from his successors about how so-and-so politicians and businessmen were calling them to go slow on the cases.

I spoke to one such officer, who is presently handling the murder cases against Gurmeet, and he corroborated what Narayanan had told me.

'I was surprised to see how blatantly, after the Congress, the BJP took support from him for the Haryana assembly elections and the Lok Sabha elections,' he said. It may be noted that in 2014, ahead of the Haryana assembly elections, the BJP's election incharge of the state, Kailash Vijayvargiya, took forty-four candidates of his party to seek the blessings of Gurmeet Ram Rahim. The Dera's PAW openly supported the BJP both in the assembly elections and the 2014 Lok Sabha elections. In the seats dominated by members of the sect, it played a vital role in the victory of BJP candidates.

'Imagine that just ten days before the verdict in the rape case against him, Haryana education minister Ram Vilas Sharma donated Rs 51 lakh from his ministry's quota to promote sports at the Dera,' the CBI officer told me. Like Narayanan, they too received calls. 'If he [Narayanan] received calls from Congress leaders, we received calls from BJP leaders, some even from ministers in the Haryana government.' Gurmeet was also appointed a brand ambassador of the 'Swachh Bharat Abhiyan' by none other than Prime Minister Narendra Modi. 'Imagine the kind of pressure we had to face to probe this rapist and murderer,' he added.

Narayanan now lives a peaceful retired life, though Gurmeet's conviction in 2017 did bring back old memories for him. He firmly believes that if any investigating agency does its job well, without buckling under threats and political pressure, the results are bound to come. Though it took almost ten years after the CBI filed the charge sheet against Gurmeet for the case to reach its logical end, even so, Narayanan said he was content with the result.

When I asked him whether he was still in touch with the two survivors, he said, 'Oh yes. Those two women are like daughters to me. They showed exemplary courage and without them, it would have been impossible to crack this case.' Narayanan said that he was still worried about the threat looming over the sadhvis who testified against Gurmeet.

'The Qurbani wing of the Dera is still active and these people are simply crazy fellows. Those two girls should always be watchful till this sect is completely disbanded.'

Convicted!

In the annals of contemporary Indian history, 25 August 2017 will be remembered as a day when a dreaded criminal and his followers held to ransom two states of the country, Punjab and Haryana, resulting in the deaths of thirty-nine people and damage to public and personal property that cost millions of rupees. The mayhem that followed the verdict against Gurmeet Singh, in which he was held guilty on two counts of rape, would raise questions about the inefficiency of the state machinery and also the role of the media and political parties, who collectively gave a criminal legitimacy and were instrumental in nurturing his larger-than-life image.

The build-up to the 25 August havoc started just a few days earlier. Reports started appearing in national newspapers that the final verdict on the rape case against the Dera chief was about to be delivered. The special CBI court in Panchkula concluded hearings in the case on 17 August and reserved pronouncing the verdict till 25 August.

By 20 August, more than fifty thousand Dera followers had reached Panchkula, and their numbers were swelling by the hour. They were camping near government buildings, in market complexes and parks and on pavements in the city. With open spaces having no toilets, the followers were defecating in the open and disposing of garbage wherever they could. The city soon smelled of rotting garbage. As per local accounts, the followers were drying their clothes on cars parked in public spaces.

The situation took on grave proportions by 23 August. Every possible nook and cranny of the city was occupied by the Dera followers. Reports started coming in that Sector 23 of Panchkula was completely under siege and that the Dera followers had started their langar and Naam Charcha there.

Followers from Sirsa, Bathinda, Mansa, Moga, Abohar, Fazilka, Sangrur, Patiala and other towns with considerable Dera influence formed the main part of this congregation. They pitched tents in any available space in the city. Near the congregation, a twenty-four-hour langar was started and stalls for medicines and other basic services were erected. This was despite the fact that a prohibitory order under Section 144 had already been imposed in the city and the large number of police and paramilitary forces were busy frisking any vehicle or bus plying on the Zirakpur–Panchkula highway. Several vehicles were stopped near Zirakpur's main chowk, but not the Dera followers walking towards the city. For the express purpose of detaining the Dera followers indulging in any kind of violence, the Sector 16 cricket stadium in Chandigarh was converted into a temporary jail.

Sensing that this massive a gathering could lead to a possible clash, most electronic media channels based out of Delhi, for some of whom Gurmeet was a source of revenue, started dispatching their crews and OB vans to Panchkula and Sirsa.

'On the road leading to Panchkula from Zirakpur, all you could see were either Dera followers or security personnel,' recalls Rajat Tandon, a senior journalist working with a national media channel who was witness to the vandalism that followed the verdict. He said that the followers outnumbered the security personnel deployed to stop them. 'Dera followers were even using adjoining farmlands to enter the city.'

By 23 August, the state administrations of Punjab and Haryana were aware, through media reports and intelligence inputs, that blood might well be spilt on the roads of Sirsa and Panchkula if the Dera followers were not contained or evicted before the verdict was pronounced.

On 23 August, I wrote a piece for Newslaundry.com with the headline 'Dera Sacha Sauda Chief's Moment of Truth on Friday'. The huge gathering of the Dera followers in Panchkula, despite prohibitory orders, was a serious cause of concern. The city seemed to be sitting on a tinderbox. I wrote in the introduction:

A sea of khaki has descended on the otherwise vibrant city of Panchkula in Haryana, turning it into a garrison town since Tuesday . . . Another cohort has also descended on the city: the Dera followers, who have laid siege to the city. Some in the hope of catching darshan of their sect leader, some to show their devotion and faith. The states of Punjab and Haryana fear the Dera devout can resort to violence if the verdict by the special CBI court goes against Singh.

Similar scenes were unfolding in Sirsa. More than ten companies of paramilitary forces were already stationed in the town. Here too, the influx of the Dera followers remained unabated. As per intelligence inputs on 25 August, more than sixty thousand Dera followers were already in the town, with most of them holed up in the two Dera premises there. Saurabh Shukla, a correspondent with NDTV, who was perhaps one of those journalists who stayed in Sirsa for the longest time both before and after the verdict, recalls, 'In my entire journalistic career, I have never seen such a heavy deployment of police and paramilitary forces. The entire town was completely sealed and fortified.'

Shukla said that at the main crossroads of Shah Satnam Chowk, the entry point to the road towards the main Dera was completely blocked. Concertina wires and cement blocks were used to barricade the road, and entry towards the Dera was strictly prohibited. The crossroads was manned by the Haryana Police personnel, backed by paramilitary personnel. Shukla said that till the morning of 25 August, the media vehicles and OB vans were excluded from this restriction. 'The media centre at the Dera was open to all the media. Followers were divided into groups of roughly two hundred people, and each group was assigned one channel. Their duty was to monitor what line that channel was taking.'

At times, things became ugly for those reporting from the Dera premises when the followers kept interrupting or waving lathis or baseball bats at the reporters and their crew.

Till 24 August, speculation was rife that the Dera chief might not visit the special CBI court in Panchkula. This was a serious cause of worry for security agencies. 'In case the verdict goes against him and he is holed up in his Dera, any attempt to arrest him would lead to the loss of many lives,' a CBI official attached to the probe told me on the morning of 24 August.

However, Gurmeet Ram Rahim tweeted at 12 noon on 24 August: *'Hamne sada kanoon ka sammaan kiya hain. Halanki hamari back mein dard hain, phir bhee kanoon ka palan karte hue ham court jaroor jaayenge. Hame bhagwan par yakeen hain. Sabhi shanti banaye rakhe.'* (I have always respected the law. Although I have back pain, I will abide by the law and will go to court. I have faith in God. Please maintain peace.)

This eased the agency's anxiety a bit, but now the real worry was—will he agree to fly directly to Panchkula or will he take the road to reach the court? With the Dera followers mapping the entire route from Sirsa to Panchkula, a road journey to the court could also become a severe law-and-order problem.

Finally, on the day of the verdict, at around 8.30 a.m., the Dera chief left for Panchkula from the Dera Sacha Sauda headquarters in Sirsa in his cavalcade, comprising more than two hundred and fifty vehicles. According to an eyewitness, many followers threw themselves in front of the cavalcade the moment it started from the Dera, in an attempt to stop it from proceeding.

'The mood of the Dera followers was charged. Thousands were seen running alongside the cavalcade. They were armed with lathis and swords. In the town itself, there was complete silence,' Saurabh Shukla recalls.

Most commercial establishments in the town were closed and people had already hoarded groceries and other essentials, anticipating large-scale violence in case the verdict went against the Dera chief. 'They feared a replay of 2007, when Dera followers and Sikhs came to blows after Gurmeet allegedly dressed as the tenth Guru of the Sikhs,' Shukla said.

The road connecting the Dera to NH-9 in Sirsa was cleared of all traffic. The cavalcade included eight SUVs with tinted glasses, and Gurmeet was in one of them. The route to be taken by the Dera chief had been submitted to the police by the Dera management in writing. The cavalcade was to move through Sirsa–Fatehabad–Bhuna–Uklana–Narwana–Kaithal–Dhand–Kurukshetra–Ambala–Dera Bassi–Zirakpur–Panchkula—all through Haryana.

By the time the cavalcade approached Zirakpur, the number of vehicles had swelled to 350. During his journey from Sirsa to Zirakpur, the Dera chief stopped at several places dominated by his followers. His close aides kept joining him in luxurious vehicles during these stopovers. Those who were witness to the huge cavalcade said it was one of the rarest sights ever to be seen.

'It looked like this man cared a hoot about the law. The expensive vehicles were moving at such high speed that some of the media persons doing live broadcasts en route barely managed to save their lives,' Rajat recalled. 'Most of the vehicles were stopped near a temple, situated a few kilometres from the court premises. A radius of roughly 500 metres, and all entry points to the courts were completely sealed.'

At around 2.18 p.m., Gurmeet Ram Rahim entered the premises of the CBI court and the hearing began at 2.30 p.m. While this was happening, the Dera followers started celebrating outside the secured radius, stating that 'Pitaji' had been acquitted of all the charges. Later, it was learnt that that was deliberately done to distract the security forces.

At around 3.05 p.m., special CBI judge Jagdeep Singh convicted Gurmeet Ram Rahim in both the rape cases and reserved the announcement of the sentence for 28 August.

According to the public prosecutor for the CBI, who was present inside the courtroom, when held guilty, the convict was not able to understand what the judge had said. Gurmeet sat with his hands folded all through the hearing. He was immediately taken into a Scorpio parked outside the court. Apprehending that the Dera followers would make trouble, the police asked him to record an appeal on camera asking his followers to maintain peace. The other vehicles in the cavalcade that had accompanied him from Sirsa to Panchkula were asked to leave the area.

As per one of the eyewitness accounts published in the *Tribune*, after the court verdict, when the Haryana Police officers took custody of the Dera head, his security team objected. The security team's members said that Gurmeet Ram Rahim would go in a private vehicle instead of a vehicle of the Haryana Police. According to the report, as the Haryana Police officers did not listen to their request, one of the security men 'slapped' and pushed an inspector general (IG) rank officer. Members of the Dera security staff then lay in front of the Haryana Police vehicle to stop it from moving. The report further said that the Haryana Police, with the help of paramilitary forces, rounded up around eight security personnel of the Dera chief and detained them in a room in the court complex. Later, this incident was confirmed to the media by the additional director general of police (ADGP) , Law and Order, Muhammad Akil, who was present at the entrance of the court complex when the incident took place. He said that the security personnel of the Dera head 'misbehaved' with Karnal IG Subhash Yadav.

After the Haryana Police managed to neutralize the security personnel of the Dera chief, he was taken to a chopper and was flown to Rohtak to be locked in a designated jail. It is a norm that those convicted by the Panchkula court are taken to the Ambala-based central jail. However, the plan was changed at the last minute after reports were received of thousands of Dera followers gathering outside Ambala jail. As the Dera has a marginal following in Rohtak, a decision was taken to lodge him there.

Meanwhile, news of the conviction started trickling out and reporters of various channels deputed near the courts went live, giving details of the verdict.

I was on my way to the Wire's office in Delhi for a Facebook Live on the same issue. I had reached India Gate when I received a message from a journalist friend who was in Panchkula. It simply said, 'Convicted.' I was overwhelmed with emotion. I asked the auto driver to stop. I stepped out and yelled with joy. I immediately realized I was crying and shaking with a sense of fulfilment. The next thing I did was to call my wife and immediately ask her to leave home with our nine-year-old daughter and go to a safer place.

Meanwhile, in Panchkula, the Dera followers started marching towards the police force. 'A rain of stones started falling on us. It was complete bedlam. The local police was seen scurrying for cover,' Rajat Tandon said, recollecting the horror.

The first report of violence by Dera followers came from Sector 3 of Panchkula, where they vandalized and set many cars on fire. Near the court, while the police were running for cover, several media vans were targeted and set ablaze. The paramilitary forces took over, firing tear-gas shells and blank shots to handle the growing crowd near the court.

By 3.30 p.m., the situation had completely spiralled out of the hands of the security forces. Widespread violence gripped Panchkula. By 4 p.m., curfew was imposed. Reports were coming in of the Dera followers entering several sectors of Panchkula on a vandalism spree.

At Hafed Chowk in the city, outnumbered by the rampaging Dera followers, the police started running away. It was a free-for-all by 4.30 p.m. News of widespread violence started coming in from districts like Mansa, Firozpur and Bathinda.

'The same Dera followers who were providing us with food and water that morning became bloodthirsty. All that came to our minds was to take cover behind military personnel,' recalls Rajat. He said that most of the offices near the court premises were set on fire by the Dera followers, and the fire brigade was struggling to douse the flames while braving the barrage of stones being pelted on them.

By the time I reached the Wire's office in Delhi, all we could see were visuals of burning vehicles and Dera followers rioting in parts of Punjab and Haryana. The security forces were struggling to control the situation. By the time I finished my Facebook Live, the death count had reached eighteen. Meanwhile, 200 injured had been shifted to General Hospital, Panchkula. More than sixty people, critically injured, were referred to other hospitals.

In Sirsa, the moment news of the verdict came in, thousands of Dera followers started marching towards Shah Satnam Chowk for a direct confrontation with the security forces. 'Senior police officers deployed near the chowk told us to rush back to the hotels,' Saurabh Shukla recalls. The followers included women armed with petrol bombs and swords. 'An attempt to lob a petrol bomb at the security personnel by a strongly built woman who had covered her face was pre-empted when a personnel of the paramilitary fired gunshots in the air.'

He said the media teams of most of the channels that were staying at a hotel near the chowk rushed back to it. Within a few minutes of their arrival, they were asked by the hotel management to vacate immediately. Saurabh Shukla said, 'They feared that the moment Dera followers found out we were staying there, they would torch the hotel. We were now on the road and solely at the mercy of our luck.'

In Sirsa, unlike Panchkula, the situation was relatively less grave as the army had already held a flag march in the city a few times before the verdict. It had managed to contain the Dera followers behind Shah Satnam Chowk and restrained them from entering the city.

'It was a night of horror for us. With no food or water, the city locked down, it was the most helpless situation,' Shukla recalls. Somehow, the media crews of different channels managed to get a place in a dharmashala with the help of a local. 'We tore off the media stickers from our cars and parked them inside Sirsa government hospital,' Shukla recalls.

I remember that by the time I reached the NDTV office at Greater Kailash in Delhi to take part in the 9 p.m.

show, the death count had already crossed thirty. After the show, when I came out, I was informed that the heat of this violence was likely to reach Delhi as well, and as a precautionary measure, Section 144 had been imposed here as well. I also received a call from an agency source who asked me to move to a safe place because now, I was one of the potential targets for the Dera followers.

As advised, I moved to an undisclosed location. On the other side, in Rohtak, Gurmeet was lodged in Sunaria jail's 'approval cell'. The lone approval cell of the jail, which can lodge twelve prisoners, had only one prisoner that night—Gurmeet Singh. He was kept in solitary confinement due to security reasons.

A prison officer, speaking to the media later, disclosed that Gurmeet had spent his first night in jail pacing inside the cell till midnight. 'He did a lot of drama and complained of uneasiness, but a medical examination by doctors found him fit.'

The morning that followed the verdict against Gurmeet was perhaps one of the worst nightmares one could wake up to. The newspapers were filled with accounts of widespread violence in Punjab and Haryana. Visuals of dead bodies lying on pavements, trains torched, burnt vehicles and other signs of mayhem were playing on news channels. A total of thirty-nine deaths were reported, out of which thirty-two took place in Panchkula and six in Sirsa. The only signs of respite were reports that in an overnight operation by the army, with assistance from the paramilitary forces, the Dera followers had been vacated from Sirsa, and reports of violence by followers in other parts of Punjab and Haryana were sporadic.

'If it were not for the army, the casualties could have crossed several hundred—the local administration and police were a complete failure,' Rajat Tandon states as a matter of fact. He, along with some other reporters, accompanied the army personnel while they were flushing out the Dera followers from Panchkula. As per reports, on the evening of 26 August, the residents had started coming out of their houses with food and water as a sign of gratitude for the army and paramilitary forces.

On the other hand, the statement of Haryana Chief Minister Manohar Lal Khattar, aired on news channel the same day, spoke volumes of the failure of the Haryana government, and he admitted that there had been lapses in managing the law-and-order situation after the verdict. There was a clamour for his resignation by opposition parties, but he preferred to carry on with his job.

In Sirsa, on 26 August, the next challenge for the security forces was to get the Dera premises vacated. As per reports, more than seventy thousand Dera followers, including senior citizens, women and children, were still inside the Dera. Four columns of the army cordoned off the Dera headquarters and started making announcements asking the Dera followers to vacate the premises with immediate effect. The paramilitary forces and state police formed a second security cordon outside the headquarters. More than hundred buses were arranged to take the followers and leave them outside the city. The security personnel also had intelligence inputs that many followers inside the Dera were armed with weapons, so they were treading cautiously to avoid any surprise attacks.

The heavy military presence soon broke the morale of the followers and they started coming out of the headquarters in hordes. During the process, the security forces recovered several licensed and unlicensed arms from the followers, which included rifles and an AK-47.

'This was also when the media got some access to Dera followers. And it was unbelievable that most of the Dera followers leaving the premises had their faith in "Pitaji" intact,' an NDTV reporter, who was present at the spot while the Dera was vacated, says. 'He is God's incarnation and it is one of his *leela*s that he has gone to jail,' a Dera follower told Shukla on camera.

With the situation in Sirsa and other parts of the two states almost under control, the Dera followers, the media and people in general were waiting and speculating about the quantum of punishment Gurmeet would get.

Sensing another backlash by the Dera followers, on 28 August, the day when the punishment was to be announced, a multilevel security arrangement was made in Rohtak and also around Sunaria jail, where the Dera chief was lodged. For this purpose, along with the state police, twenty-three companies of paramilitary forces were deployed. A special courtroom was set up inside the Sunaria jail for the pronouncement of the sentence. Special CBI judge Jagdeep Singh was flown from Panchkula in a chopper that landed in the jail premises.

The judge allotted ten minutes to both sides to present their arguments. The prosecution demanded the maximum punishment for the rape convict, but the defence argued that the Dera chief was a social worker who had worked for the welfare of the people. The defence lawyer cited several examples of his social work and urged the judge to take a lenient view. He also cited Gurmeet's health problems and the ailments of his aged mother.

However, putting aside the defence counsel's pleas, the court observed that the Dera head had behaved like a beast and thus deserved no mercy. It stated that when the convict did not spare his own pious disciples and acted like a wild beast, he did not deserve any mercy. It added that the victims revered Gurmeet Ram Rahim Singh as God, but he committed a breach of the gravest nature. It observed that a man 'who has neither any concern for humanity nor any mercy in his nature does not deserve leniency. Such a criminal act by one who is stated to be heading a religious organization is bound to shatter the image of pious and sacred, spiritual, social, cultural and religious institutions existing in the country since time immemorial.'

Finally, the court awarded ten years each for the rape of the two women, and made it clear that the punishment would run consequently. The court also imposed a fine of Rs 15 lakh on the Dera chief in each of the cases, and ordered that both victims should get Rs 14 lakh each as compensation.

The moment the quantum of punishment was announced, the Dera chief, who had maintained the image of a superhero for years, broke down in tears. He dropped to the floor and held on to his chair to stop the marshals from escorting him out of the courtroom. Media reports suggest that he reportedly kept pleading with the judge to 'please forgive him'. He was finally dragged out as he refused to leave the makeshift court premises, complaining of chest pain and high blood pressure. A medical examination, however, deemed him to be fit. He was soon given a jail uniform and lodged in a cell.

Someone once known for his flamboyant lifestyle, revered as a god by lakhs of followers, and someone who allegedly had several powerful politicians and members of the media in his pocket, Gurmeet was henceforth going to be known as *qaidi* (prisoner) number 1997 by his fellow inmates in Rohtak jail.

Sources

The sources of various statements mentioned in the book:

- Statement of one of the two sadhvis subjected to rape:

In the court of A.K. Verma, additional sessions judge, Ambala:
CBI case no. 11, dated 27 October 2007.
FIR no. RC-5 (S)/2002/SIU-XV/CHG, dated 12 December 2002.
Recorded under Sections 376, 506 and 509 IPC, police station:
SCB, CBI, Chandigarh.
The information sheet and deposition of a witness on oath.

CBI versus Gurmeet Ram Rahim Singh
FIR no. RC-5 (S)/2002/SIU-XV/CHG, dated 12 December 2002.
Principal Witness 10: the information sheet and deposition
of Shyama, aged around thirty-five years, employed, r/o
Chandigarh.

- Document related to ex-army personnel imparting arms
  training to the Dera followers:

Document no. 117/1/GSI.
A copy of HQ 10 Information Division letter no. 1551/GSI, dated 13 December 2010.

- Details of Suman's and Khatta Singh's statements, also details of the murders of Ranjit Singh and Ram Chander Chhatrapati derived from sources:

  ○ Copy of the original anonymous letter sent to various authorities in 2002.
  ○ Copy of the FIR of the CBI case no. 5/S/02-SIU-XV/, Chandigarh, dated 12 January 2002, along with a copy of the high court order dated 24 September 2002.
  ○ Statement of Khatta Singh, s/o Jhanda Singh, r/o Kothi no. 2, Shah Satnam Nagar, Sirsa. Recorded under Section 164 CrPC by Balwinder Kumar, judicial magistrate first class, Chandigarh.
  ○ Statement of Suman. Recorded under Section 164 of the CrPC by the chief judicial magistrate, Chandigarh, on 19 March 2007.
  ○ Original FIR of case no. RC-8(S)/2003/SCb/CHG, dated 9 December 2003.

- Details of case related to Vishwas Gupta:

Criminal miscellaneous petition no. M-30392 of 2011 in the Punjab and Haryana High Court at Chandigarh.

- Charges of castration levelled by Hansraj via a civil writ petition filed in the Punjab and Haryana High Court at Chandigarh in 2012 by the counsel of petitioner, Navkiran Singh.

Acknowledgements

This book would not have been possible if one braveheart journalist, Ram Chander Chhatrapati, had not taken the lead in making public the gory details of the Dera Sacha Sauda. I have immense respect for him for embodying the highest ideals of journalism. I am immensely indebted to his family, particularly his son, Anshul Chhatrapati, who relentlessly fought for justice despite pressure and threats, and helped me with documents and leads related to the case.

I have the highest regard for the two rape survivors, who showed extraordinary courage in recording their testimony with the CBI. Their statements led to the conviction of Gurmeet Ram Rahim.

My special thanks to Mulinja Narayanan and Hansraj, for providing insights and details which helped me understand how a nexus of politicians and law-enforcement agencies shielded Gurmeet Ram Rahim for years.

I thank *Tehelka*, Harinder Baweja and Ethmad Khan for planning, executing and bringing the first investigation into the Dera to a logical end in 2007.

I am also grateful to Hartosh for agreeing to write the Foreword. A journalist of his calibre adds immense value to the book

To all those unnamed sources who helped us from time to time, with documents and leads, my heartfelt gratitude.

At Penguin Random House, I owe a special thanks to Swati Chopra who commissioned the book, encouraged me during its writing and helped me through the process of publication. And thanks to Shanuj for adding finesse to it.

The ten years since the story first broke were not easy for me. From facing threats to my family to the frustration I felt seeing Gurmeet Ram Rahim free, was an ordeal. Thanks, Yasha, for staying by my side and for being my rock-solid buddy. The credit goes to you for keeping me sane.